THE HANOI MARCH

American POWs in North Vietnam's Crucible

GARY WAYNE FOSTER

HELLGATE PRESS   ASHLAND, OREGON

THE HANOI MARCH: AMERICAN POWs IN NORTH VIETNAM'S
CRUCIBLE
Published by Hellgate Press
(An imprint of L&R Publishing, LLC)

Hellgate Press
PO Box 3531
Ashland, OR 97520
email: sales@hellgatepress.com

Cover & Interior Design: L. Redding
ISBN: 978-1-954163-35-5

Printed and bound in the United States of America
First edition 10 9 8 7 6 5 4 3 2 1

By the end of June 1966, two years into the Vietnam air war that would last for another six and a half years, the North Vietnamese shot down and captured one hundred American airmen. Of these, fifty were paraded through the streets of Hanoi during the evening of 6 July 1966. This is a true account of that event.

Dedicated to and in Honor of Those Fifty Americans

Everett Alvarez, Jr.
Thomas Joseph Barrett
James Franklin Bell
Kile Dag "Red" Berg
Cole Black
Charles Graham "Chuck" Boyd
Edward Alan Brudno
Richard Marvin "Skip" Brunhaver
Alan Leslie Brunstrom
Arthur William Burer
Phillip Neal Butler
Ronald Edward Byrne, Jr.
Gerald Leonard "Jerry" Coffee
Arthur Cormier
Render Crayton
Edward A. Davis
Jeremiah Andrew "Jerry" Denton, Jr.
Robert Bartsch Doremus
Jerry Donald Driscoll
John Howard "Howie" Dunn
Leonard Corbett Eastman
Ralph Ellis Gaither, Jr.
Paul Edward Galanti
Lawrence Nicholas "Larry" Guarino
Porter Alexander Halyburton

Carlyle Smith "Smitty" Harris
David Burnett Hatcher
James Otis Hivner
James Leo "Duffy" Hutton
Paul Anthony Kari
Richard Paul "Pop" Keirn
Hayden James Lockhart, Jr.
Alan Pierce Lurie
John Bryan "JB" McKamey
Raymond James Merritt
Robert Delayney Peel
Robert Baldwin "Percy" Purcell
Darrel Edwin Pyle
Richard Raymond "Dick" Ratzlaff
Jon A. Reynolds
James Robinson "Robbie" Risner
Wendell Burke "Wendy" Rivers
Wesley Duane Schierman
Bruce Gibson Seeber
William Leonard Shankel
Robert Harper Shumaker
Jerry Allen Singleton
Larry Howard Spencer
Ronald Edward Storz
William Michael Tschudy

And also, Murphy Neal Jones

THE HANOI MARCH

CONTENTS

PART ONE
Setting and Players

PART TWO
The Gathering

PART THREE
Parades and Other Displays

PART FOUR
The Hanoi March

PART FIVE
Witnesses

PART SIX
Antecedent and Fallout

PART SEVEN
Retrospect

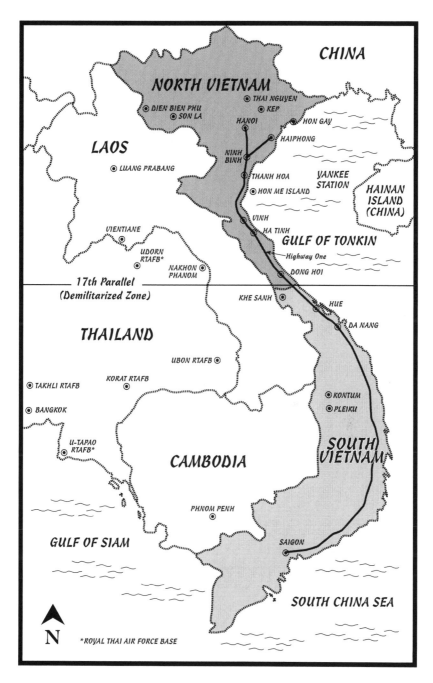

General Map of the Southeast Asia Theater, 1966

THE HANOI MARCH

ABBREVIATIONS AND INFORMATION

AAA – Anti-Aircraft Artillery (Triple- A)

BARCAP – Barrier Combat Air Patrol (air protection)

BN – Bombardier/Navigator

CAG – Airwing Commander (Navy)

CAP – Combat Air Patrol (covering protection)

CV/CVA/CVN – Aircraft Carrier Designation (Navy)

CVW – Airwing Designation (Navy)

DMZ – Demilitarized Zone (marked by the Ben Hai River)

KIA – Killed in Action

MIA – Missing in Action

MIGCAP – MiG Combat Air Patrol (enemy aircraft protection)

MiG – Russian Fighter Jet

NFO – Naval Flight Officer

NVA – North Vietnamese Army

NVN – North Vietnam

POL – Petroleum, Oil, Lubricants

POW – Prisoner of War

PSO – Pilot/Systems Officer (precursor to the WSO - Air Force)

RAG – Replacement Air Group (Navy)

RIO – Radio Intercept Officer (F-4B, Navy)

RTAFB – Royal Thai Air Force Base

RVAH – Heavy Reconnaissance Attack Squadron (Navy)

SAM – Surface-to-Air Missile.

SRO – Senior Ranking Officer

SVN – South Vietnam

TFS – Tactical Fighter Squadron (Air Force)

VA – Attack Squadron (Navy)

VF – Fighter Squadron (Navy)

WSO – Weapons Systems Officer (F-4C)

U.S. Fixed-wing Aircraft (Fighters, Bombers, Fighter-Bombers and Reconnaissance Aircraft)

Navy
A-1	Skyraider
A-3	Skywarrior
A-4	Skyhawk
A-6	Intruder
F-8/RF-8	Crusader
RA-5C	Vigilante

Air Force
F-100	Supersabre
F-101	Voodoo
F-105	Thunderchief
O-1	Birddog (spotter plane)

Common to Air Force, Navy and Marines
F-4	Phantom

North Vietnam Fixed-wing Aircraft
MiG-17	Fresco
MiG-21	Fishbed

Translation

Pho is Vietnamese for street. In this account, each word is interchangeable with the other. *Pho Trang Tien* is the same as Trang Tien Street. *Pho* is also the name of a noodle soup. It is pronounced "Phuh." Diacritic and tonal marks have been omitted from Vietnamese words for ease of reading.

PART ONE

SETTINGS AND PLAYERS

THE HANOI MARCH

CHAPTER 1

HON GAY

On his second tour with the fleet, both on the USS *Constellation* (CV-64), Lieutenant (j.g.) Everett Alvarez, a twenty-six-year-old native of Salinas, California, and other pilots in a flight of ten A-4C Skyhawks launched from the aircraft carrier at 2:30 p.m. on the fifth of August 1964. The A-4s of attack squadron VA-144, commonly called the Roadrunners, rendezvoused over the carrier above the Gulf of Tonkin and flew in a northerly direction toward the coast of North Vietnam.

At thirty thousand feet, the single-engine jets caught up with a flight of propeller-driven A-1 Skyraider attack planes, also from *Constellation*, flying at a lower altitude. Due to their slower speed, the A-1s launched well before the A-4s.

In reprisal for what came to be called the Gulf of Tonkin incident, *Constellation*'s A-4s and A-1s attacked a North Vietnamese naval base at Hon Gay northeast of Haiphong.

Alvarez participated in a previous mission the night before to protect two U.S. destroyers from threats made by the North Vietnamese navy. He carried flares for illumination. Due to low cloud cover, the flight proved hazardous, but all planes recovered on *Constellation*.

Now, on his second mission in as many days, as he neared the target, Alvarez rolled in and fired rockets in a salvo. Other A-4s followed. They destroyed several torpedo boats. Alvarez made a pass with his 20mm cannon aimed at a larger ship. The Skyhawk's bullets hit the water, marched up the side of the ship and smashed through the bridge area. Chunks of metal flew off the ship.

During the air attack, North Vietnamese gun crews zeroed in on the lone A-4. Machine-gun fire, more intense than Alvarez anticipated, swept past his cockpit. Exploding projectiles from heavy anti-aircraft artillery rocked his plane. Then, finding their mark, enemy shells ripped the guts from beneath Alvarez's plane.

"I've been hit," Alvarez said into his microphone as he jettisoned the ordnance racks under his wings to reduce drag.

The Skyhawk banked to the left. Alvarez spoke into his mic.

"I'm on fire. No control."

And, not even a few seconds later, "I'm getting out!"

Alvarez had no option but to eject. He was over water but unfortunately, near the coastline.

As soon as he splashed down, Alvarez heard rifle shots and was nicked by a bullet. Soon captured, he was hauled aboard a North Vietnamese fishing vessel.

Alvarez was transferred to a much larger boat that drew alongside. The crew members asked if he was Vietnamese (from South Vietnam). Alvarez, responding in Spanish, said he didn't understand. Through further questioning and after having looked at his identification card and equipment stenciled with the name of the aircraft carrier, a man asked Alvarez if he was *My* (pronounced "me"). Alvarez indicated again his lack of comprehension. The man wrote the word *My* on a piece of paper and next to it, USA. With an inquiring face, the man pointed at the letters, then at Alvarez. He opened his hand, gesturing a question.

Alvarez, knowing they had the goods on him, admitted who he was.

The North Vietnamese, wide-eyed, stepped back in shock. They had just captured a *Phi Cong My*, an American pilot!

Alvarez was quarantined in a cell near Hon Gay for several days where he was treated relatively well. He met a pleasant, helpful man who spoke English. He was given bowls of soup consisting of chicken heads and buffalo hooves in boiling brown water, but so disgusting, Alvarez couldn't stomach the food.

The next day, Alvarez, worried about what may happen to him, met an officer who would soon be referred to as Owl due to his resemblance with the nocturnal bird. The questioning began: What was the mission? Will there be more attacks? When? Where?

The young U.S. Navy pilot didn't answer.

Alvarez spent a couple of nights in various locations before he was driven to Hanoi. Several days later, bound and blindfolded, he entered the main gate of a prison called Hoa Lo located on a street with the same name.

Five months after the Hon Gay attack, in January 1965, *Constellation*, leaving Alvarez behind, departed the Gulf of Tonkin and sailed for San Diego.

* * * *

Everett Alvarez was the first American pilot captured in North Vietnam and incarcerated in its main prison during what came to be called the Vietnam War.*

Within six weeks after Alvarez was shot down, U.S. combat aircraft began deploying to airbases in South Vietnam, Thailand, Guam, the Philippines and on aircraft carriers sent to an area referred to as Yankee Station in the Gulf of Tonkin.

The downing of Alvarez over Hon Gay in 1964 marked the beginning of a long line of captured American airmen. By late June 1966, America had lost hundreds of planes and many of its best pilots. The American prisoner-of-war ranks in North Vietnam were being filled by established, well-educated career officers with many years of flight training and experience. Whereas the average age of American fighting men in South Vietnam was twenty, the

---

*During WWII, America lost over 400 airmen in Vietnam while fighting military forces from Japan. Many of these airmen were held captive by the Japanese.

average age of incarcerated American airmen, some having served in World War II and Korea, was thirty-two.

Flying high, brought low, a certain mawkishness among airmen shot down over North Vietnam, was common. God-like in their airplanes while slipping through the clouds, the masters of the sky were in fact mere mortals.

Every shootdown was different as were the locations where the airmen, if they survived, were captured. Downed airmen made attempts to hide and escape. Some evaded capture and were rescued, but many weren't. Restricted by the terrain or overwhelmed by their pursuers, those not rescued could not last long.

Flying into combat was nerve wracking enough. Ejecting at night from a flaming aircraft over dark, unknown terrain was terrifying. The impulse of the explosion of the ejection propellant under their seats, then the immediate impact of wind at several hundred miles per hour left aviators stunned or unconscious. Many experienced incapacitating spine, shoulder and arm injuries due to the immediate thrust of the seat ejection system. Yet, more bodily harm awaited them.

Once captured on the ground in North Vietnam, mostly in the jungles, Americans tasted the shocking, disorienting reality of a hostile environment in an alien land.

As with Everett Alvarez, some pilots who found themselves in the hands of the North Vietnamese became household names. They came to the forefront of America's consciousness and embodied the American prisoners' struggle to survive and return home.

The early names carried the banner and fame of the prisoners' plight to the end. The Americans incarcerated in Hanoi and elsewhere in North Vietnam assumed the descriptor of POW for the rest of the war and the rest of their lives.

CHAPTER 2

INSIDE THE RED RIVER

Situated in the Red River delta, the area that would become Ha Noi can be characterized today as it could have been thousands of years ago as a vast, uninterrupted plain.

Modern day archaeological digs unearthed pottery, bronze tools, stone axes and other artifacts which confirmed that as early as 2000 BC, primitive communities occupied the area. Residents lived in loosely connected clusters of huts.

Other ancient findings suggest the area may have been inhabited as early as twenty thousand years ago.

In 218 BC, Thuc Phan built a fortified settlement along the banks of the Red River but lost control of the area to invading Chinese who ruled it for centuries.

In the ninth century AD, a formidable citadel named Dai La was completed by Gao Pian.

Emperor Ly Thai To, the ruler of Hue, several hundred miles south, invoking Thuc Phan's proud history of local resistance, marched his troops north and captured Dai La. He renamed the citadel Thang Long, meaning the dragon that soars.

Ly Thai To's rule and that of the subsequent Ly dynasty lasted several hundred years.

In the seventeenth century, Thang Long, now a thriving city under the new Le dynasty, became Dong Kinh, from which the rhyming word Tonkin was derived.

After several regime changes, Gia Long, emperor of the later ruling Nguyen dynasty, designated Dong Kinh as Thang Tinh. Further, the emperor gave the country its current name. He wanted to call the land Nam Viet but instead, named it Viet Nam.

In 1831, Minh Mang, a subsequent emperor of the continuing Nguyen dynasty, gave a new name to Thang Tinh. He named it Ha Noi, which, like Viet Nam, was two words in the Vietnamese language.

Ha Noi, as with the same city with prior names, sits just west of the Song Hong on the side farthest from the Gulf of Tonkin, literally, as the city's new name translates, inside the Red River.

The eventual sweep of European exploration in the 1800s resulted in conquests of foreign regions in faraway places. As a result, a new people the Vietnamese called *Nguoi Phap* came to the eastern coast of Southeast Asia. They were of course the French. Their early explorations along the Red River in the north and the Mekong River in the south congealed France's interest in a land that held vast natural resources.

In 1859, the French occupied the southern city of Saigon. Over the next few years, France, its representatives now assuming more authority, seized additional regions in the south. However, Ha Noi and the Red River area remained beyond their grasp. In November 1873, French expeditionary forces under the leadership of Francis Garnier captured the citadel at Ha Noi.

The Vietnamese enlisted support from the so-called Black Flag army, a gang of ruthless bandits of Chinese origin, to fight the French intrusion.

A month after Francis Garnier defeated the citadel's forces, the fort was attacked by Black Flag. Garnier was killed in battle, his head severed not far from the fortress walls.

Vietnamese leaders, realizing the Europeans were not going to leave Tonkin, agreed to a treaty with the French in 1874. As a result, France gained limited access to the Ha Noi region, securing a tenuous foothold on Indochina's northern waterway.

Almost a decade later in April 1882, the French stormed the

walls of Ha Noi's ancient citadel again. Henri Riviere, the commander, captured it within an hour. Later, in May 1883, Riviere met his death at the battle of Cau Giay (Paper Bridge) just outside Ha Noi.

On the sixth of June 1884, France and Viet Nam signed the more binding *Traité de Patenotre*. Named after France's Minister to China Jules Patenotre, the treaty gave France control of Cochin, Annam and Tonkin. Ha Noi would be the capital of *Indochine du temps des Français*.

The importance of controlling Ha Noi was always of paramount, if not paranoidal concern for the Vietnamese, but even more so now for French colonialists. Nonetheless, France's particular interest in the Red River as a trading corridor and medium with northern Viet Nam grew.

Suspicion and hostility toward the French seethed but France wasted no time. Ships flying *le drapeau tricolore*, the bold red, white and blue flag of France, arrived in increasing numbers carrying abundant resources. Much to the chagrin of the Vietnamese, France also sent thousands of soldiers, merchants and administrators to Indochina. The French, importing their cultural values and technical and administrative skills, created a seemingly viable government and a vibrant social fabric for themselves.

Accelerated development plans served the needs of the French who desired to make Vietnam, now one word, albeit all of Indochina, an enduring colony for the benefit and glory of the metropole of France . . . forever.

Hanoi, also becoming one word, experienced a significant reformation. Under the guiding hand of planners and architects, the French constructed railroads, streets and highways, canals and irrigation and drainage networks. They built communication, commercial and administrative systems, ports, industrial areas, sanitation facilities, schools and hospitals.

The French were intent to bring the majesty of Paris to Hanoi through an unspoken *politique de prestige*. Imposing buildings with stylish French doors and big, prestigious porte-cochere entrances to inviting courtyards, became prevalent.

Villas followed the French concept of large front yards, not to be used so much as admired, and small backyards with outhouses and servant quarters. Spacious and airy, elegant homes with verandas, grand foyers, intricate inlay and tile-work and sweeping staircases elicited the grandeur and importance of their French inhabitants.

The French saw a rare opportunity of working in an unexploited laboratory ripe for architectural experimentation. The designers' blending of French neo-classical styles, emerging at the beginning of the 1900s, was uniquely refined for Vietnam and worked to produce a cosmopolitan aura of sophistication and elan.

Paul Doumer pushed the city further. Under his direction, l'hotel de ville (city hall), la mairie (city court house), the university and government ministries, unique in their style, exhibited indisputable French authority and permanence.

The shock of the city's ochre-colored administration buildings, not high in elevation but built with large shuttered windows and ceiling fans in each room, exuded an exotic, tropical drama. The same strange, even nauseating paint characterized the façade of the governor-general's mansion that marked a prominent corner of what would become Ba Dinh Square. The color of the stately building, designed by Henri Vildieu, surrounded by lush vegetation of the botanical gardens, soon came to define the city's welcoming grace.

The Hanoi Opera House, a majestic edifice built between 1902 and 1911, provided tangible proof of the French perpetuating their influence through *la culture Française.*

A nineteen-span, steel lattice bridge, French Indochina's response to the Eiffel Tower, spanned the muddy Red River. Appropriately, it was given the name Le Pont Paul Doumer (Paul Doumer Bridge) which Doumer himself described as the most significant structure ever built in Asia.

Unfortunately, Hanoi and its environs suffered from the effects of hundreds of stagnant lakes and ponds and disease-infested marshes abandoned by the millennial meanderings of the Red River. During the late 1800s, thousands of workers, called coolies, each using *quang ganh*, a pole over the shoulder from which at each end a basket of dirt hung, formed a continuous line of human dump trucks and filled in the lakes and ponds. The French eradicated the malaria-ridden swamps and much of the health menace.

Ancient and colonial Hanoi developed around an oblong body of water the French called La Petit Lac. Known locally as the lake of the rising sword and home to giant, three-hundred-year-old turtles, the fetid lake was drained, cleaned and allowed to refill. The lake's celebrated turtles were spared.

Large, verdant gardens and public parks radiated a leisurely colonial lifestyle at its elegant, cultural best.

Svelte, silky-haired Vietnamese women dressed in sensuous *Ao Dai*, wearing conical hats and carrying *quang ganh* with ripe fruit or colorful tropical flowers in its baskets, captured the imagination of every European artist.

Not surprisingly, the French considered Hanoi to be *le Paris de l'est*, a description also, but less formally ascribed to its rival city Saigon, a thousand miles south.

Incomparable in size to Paris, Hanoi never reached the significance of Singapore, Hong Kong or Shanghai. But with its special charm, as depicted in early postcards, the city lured scientists, romantics, writers, and the adventurous. Hanoi, the capital of Tonkin and the larger *Indochine*, became a paradise in Asia.

But all was not well in paradise.

Revenue from agricultural exports, especially opium, wasn't enough. France was obliged to cough up additional funding, causing officials to ask the question: What do the buggers do out there?

To authorities back home in France, Hanoi was too pretentious, especially for an upstart colony located so far away.

In contrast, the indigenous people thought the French and their developments were arrogant, intrusive and insulting. Discontent among the Vietnamese spread. The embers of self-rule burned intensely.

Although generations of French grew up in Hanoi with the guarantee of a continuing colonial lifestyle *outre-mer*, France's dominance in Hanoi and its rule over Vietnam would last less than one hundred years.

CHAPTER 3

USAF 67TH TACTICAL FIGHTER SQUADRON – KORAT, THAILAND

During its two temporary deployments to Korat Royal Thai Air Base in 1965, the United States Air Force 67th Tactical Fighter Squadron (TFS), the proud Fighting Cocks, suffered the effects of combat in North Vietnam. Created in 1943, the squadron, equipped now with F-105 Thunderchief fighter jets, was home-based at Kadena on Okinawa to where it would return after each deployment.

On 2 March 1965, just days after the first deployment of the 67th TFS to Korat, the U.S. Air Force launched its first Rolling Thunder strike against North Vietnam. The Fighting Cocks lost three F-105s in the space of two hours. The pilots parachuted and were rescued.

On 22 March, Lieutenant Colonel Robinson "Robbie" Risner, the squadron commander, flew a mission against a radar site near the coastal city of Vinh.

Robbie Risner was born in 1925 and raised in Tulsa, Oklahoma. He joined the Air Force in 1943. Risner flew the P-38, P-39, P-40 and P-51 fighters in World War II and the F-86 in Korea where in one incident he chased a MiG at near supersonic speed between two hangers before shooting it down. Risner downed eight MiGs, becoming an Ace after five.

Now, over North Vietnam, Risner's F-105 was hit by anti-aircraft fire. He flew his crippled Thunderchief over the Gulf of Tonkin and ejected. He was rescued and flown back to Korat to rejoin his unit.

Although suffering no casualties so far, the downing of Risner's aircraft resulted in the squadron's fourth aircraft loss in North Vietnam.

On 3 April 1965, the squadron attacked the Ham Rong Bridge at Thanh Hoa for the first time. Although the bridge sustained significant damage, it was still useable. On that mission, Risner's F-105 was hit again. He flew the aircraft to Da Nang, South Vietnam where he made an emergency landing. For the second time, Risner was immediately flown back to Thailand.

Next day, on the fourth of April 1965, Captain Carlyle "Smitty" Harris, born on 11 April 1929 in Tupelo, Mississippi, lifted off from Korat. Harris was part of a second-strike effort again to destroy the Ham Rong Bridge. The attack was led by Robbie Risner, the same pilot shot down and rescued two weeks earlier and who made an emergency landing at Da Nang the day before.

Harris and his wingman took the lead and dove for the bridge. They attacked first so the flight leader could spot the bombs. As Harris rolled into his dive, the dark steel truss of the Ham Rong Bridge filled the front of his windscreen. Harris's sight picture was clear, his attack angle good, the target dead ahead. Harris checked his airspeed and, at the right altitude, released his bombs. Harris, his plane free of its load, bottomed out of the dive. As he climbed away, his F-105 was hit in the engine by an explosive 37mm shell, the size of a lemon. The plane streamed a long tongue of bright red-orange flames.

Others in the flight warned Harris.

"Smitty, you're on fire, you're on fire!"

Harris headed east, but never made the Gulf of Tonkin. He jettisoned the canopy and fired the ejection seat. The ejection was so quick, it broke his left shoulder, but the pain didn't register in Harris's mind. He landed near a village not far from Thanh Hoa.

The villagers completely stripped him of his flight suit, boots and all his survival gear. Harris refused to give up his wedding band. Two men wrenched it from Harris's finger while acute pain from his shoulder injury shot through his entire body.

Captain Harris, now tied up, became a public spectacle. He eventually arrived in Hanoi.

Smitty Harris brought with him the Tap Code, a simple method of non-verbal communication that revolutionized the way American prisoners in Hanoi would communicate with each other.

The first deployment of the 67th TFS ended on 26 April 1965. The squadron rotated back to Kadena, but four months later, on 16 August, its planes and men re-deployed to Korat.

* * * *

A Washington native from St. John, Captain Wesley Duane Schierman was born on 21 July 1935. He was awarded his aviator wings at the end of flight training in 1956. In 1959, he received a B.S. degree in psychology from Washington State University. Schierman met his wife at university and they soon married. They had two children.

An ingratiating man with an enormous sense of humor, Wes Schierman was loyal to his country, proud of his family and equally proud of his military service.

He served with the Washington Air National Guard from 1956 to 1962. He was also a co-pilot for Northwest Airlines. In September 1962, he returned to active duty in the USAF on a three-year contract.

In early 1965, Schierman flew with the 67th Tactical Fighter Squadron during its first deployment to Korat. Upon turning twenty-nine in July 1965, Schierman agreed to a second three-month temporary duty assignment again with the 67th TFS on its second deployment to Thailand.

In late August, Wes Schierman was tasked with planning a mission to bomb military barracks near Son La, one hundred twenty-five miles west of Hanoi. Each F-105 was to carry five-hundred-pound MK-82 "Snakeye" bombs which have four square, flat metal fins designed to pop out when released. Dropped from low level, the extended fins, now perpendicular to the bomb's body, retard its descent thereby allowing the plane to depart the area prior to the bomb blast. This was to be the first mission for the F-105 using this type of bomb.

Due to the configuration of the large fins, the aerodynamics tended to cause the bombs to roll into the fuselage once released, especially if they were attached to the plane's centerline hardpoints.

During the evening of 27 August, Schierman, confident of his planning, fell into his bunk.

Up early on the twenty-eighth, the day of the raid, Schierman received weather information and briefed the mission pilots. Take off was scheduled for 0900. Schierman would be flying a two-seat F-105F.

After refueling over Laos, Schierman closed up the formation. The flight descended through cloud cover and navigated to a point just west of the airfield at Na San.

Flying at four hundred feet above ground in rough mountain terrain, at four hundred-fifty miles per hour, Schierman saw the target off his left wing about one mile south of a highway.

The second element leader dropped first, then Schierman and his wingman made their drop. They came back around on a strafing pass.

Schierman's gun jammed. He heard a heavy metallic sound to his left, followed almost immediately by a loud explosion in the aft section of the airplane. He depressed the transmit button on his radio.

"Elm lead's got problems."

The flight's number four pilot called, "Hey lead, you've got fire coming out the back. Man, it's burning."

"Yeah, I know."

Schierman ejected.

A sharp pain darted through his lower back. Simultaneously, the force of the wind hit him like a wall. Seconds later, he felt the opening of the parachute.

Schierman hit the ground hard on his back near the top of a small, denuded hill. Regaining his breath, Schierman discovered he was cut and bleeding profusely. His knees were already swelling. He made survival-radio contact with his flight and was advised a helicopter was on its way. The flight would stay with him as long as the planes had fuel. Schierman knew the flight would have to leave soon.

Schierman heard Vietnamese coming up the hill and was soon surrounded by a platoon of soldiers carrying automatic weapons. The soldiers took Schierman's boots and stripped off his gear just as the rescue helicopter appeared on the horizon.

The Vietnamese tied Schierman's arms behind him and started running him downhill through the brush. He tripped and fell several times before reaching cover in the dense jungle.

The captured airman was bound and kept in a small cave for the next seventy-two hours without food or water. Then, tied up in the back of a truck, he spent the next three nights on the road. Wes Schierman arrived in downtown Hanoi on 3 September 1965 where he entered Hanoi's prison system.

Schierman's downing was the first aircraft loss for the 67th TFS during its second deployment. Two of the squadron's pilots were now incarcerated in North Vietnam.

* * * *

Born on 19 November 1928 in Brooklyn but raised in Great Neck, New York, Ronald Edward Byrne, Jr. graduated from public high school and entered the Merchant Marine Academy. He left after three years to study law. The Korean War draft caused him to enlist in the U.S. Air Force. He received his wings and commission as a second lieutenant in 1952.

During the Korean conflict, Byrne flew seventy-five combat missions in the F-86 Sabre. After Korea, he was stationed at, among other bases, England Air Force Base where his wife gave birth to twin sons, his and his wife's first children.

Byrne received a B.S. degree in mechanical engineering from Oklahoma State University where his family was blessed with a third son.

Beginning in 1961, Ron Byrne served on the Titan missile program in California for two years. His family grew to include a fourth son. In 1964, Ron Byrne checked out in a trainer version of the F-105 and was assigned to the 67th Tactical Fighter Squadron.

On 29 August 1965, one day after Wes Schierman was shot down and captured, Major Byrne and three other pilots took off from Korat in their Thunderchiefs on their way to North Vietnam. The combat mission, Byrne's twenty-seventh, would not go entirely as planned or hoped.

In the air headed north, the flight refueled over Laos, then proceeded toward an area eighty miles northwest of Hanoi. Thirty minutes later, the four F-105s rolled in on their target, an ammunition depot at Yen Bai.

Major Byrne's fighter-bomber sustained damage from anti-aircraft fire. Flames began to shoot from the plane. Byrne continued on and delivered his bombs on target. By then, ammunition for the Thunderchief's nose-mounted machine gun was exploding. White fire and toxic fumes quickly swept into the cockpit. Byrne's plane began to plummet.

Having achieved one-third of the coveted goal of one hundred combat missions over North Vietnam, which added to his seventy-five Korea missions, Byrne reached for the ejection handle and triggered it.

The ejection system's parachute deployed rapidly with a loud clap. Byrne landed in a bamboo forest and, like a sugar cube dropped on an anthill, among swarming villagers and militia.

Ron Byrne, thirty-six years old, ended up in Hanoi to join his squadron mates Smitty Harris and Wes Schierman.

* * * *

The Fighting Cocks were plagued with two more shootdowns, one each on 31 August and 6 September for a total of four aircraft lost in combat so far during the second deployment. The two pilots were rescued.

Days later, the squadron suffered a major setback that simultaneously benefitted the North Vietnamese. A trophy unexpectedly landed in their laps.

On 16 September 1965, during his second deployment to Korat, Robbie Risner's luck ran out. His F-105 was stricken for a third time while attacking a surface-to-air missile site. Robbie Risner, an experienced horseman, still the squadron commander, ejected northeast of Thanh Hoa. Upon landing, he tore the ligaments in his knee and was disabled.

Risner's capture was cause for celebration among North Vietnamese anti-aircraft gun crews and a prize possession of North Vietnam's Air Defense Command. Since they had access to *Time* magazine depicting Risner on the cover of the April 23, 1965 issue, five months before, he became a much sought-after prize: *We've been expecting you, Mr. Risner.*

Now, they got him!

* * * *

Raymond Merritt, born on 7 October 1929 and raised in the San Gabriel Valley, attended Pasadena City College. Merritt joined the U.S. Air Force and rose to become an officer through the cadet program. He earned his wings soon thereafter. Merritt served his country in Korea where he flew one hundred missions in a Republic F-84 jet.

Ray Merritt went to Vietnam with Robbie Risner and the 67th Tactical Fighter Squadron in August 1965.

On the same raid as Robbie Risner near Thanh Hoa, and not even thirty seconds after Risner was downed, Merritt's F-105 was in trouble. On his fortieth combat mission in Vietnam, Merritt didn't hear or feel anything abnormal, but his Thunderchief was suddenly pointing to the ground. Major Merritt ejected and parachuted to earth and was immediately captured.

The 67th TFS lost two more F-105s within four days of Risner and Merritt's shootdowns. The pilots were killed.

The squadron returned to its home base of Kadena on 23 October 1965. The Fighting Cocks never returned to Vietnam.

A heavy price to pay, the 67th Tactical Fighter Squadron lost thirteen F-105 Thunderchiefs, five on the first deployment, eight on the second; and two pilots killed in action. The squadron also left five men behind in Hanoi.

CHAPTER 4

MAIN STREET – RUE PAUL BERT

Not in character with the street layout in Paris but serving as the backbone of Hanoi's European quarter, French master planners constructed four broad parallel streets with wide sidewalks in the late 1800s.

Boulevards Rollandes, Carreau and Gambetta, each running east-west, became arteries of Hanoi and facilitated a grid of intersections and perpendicular side streets.

Rue Paul Bert, the fourth and most northern parallel boulevard, blended straight on with Rue de l'Exposition. It connected the downtown to the residential area of French Hanoi. The street assumed many nicknames: Copper Street, Money Street (due to the proliferation of money changers) and Book Street.

In 1883, Rue Paul Bert, not without detractors, was described by *l'Avenir du Tonkin* (The Future of Tonkin) as a rotten sewer.

A later article described the street as being wide with a few European homes and Chinese shops. It was considered clean but commercial stores were cheapened by unsavory liquor merchants and shady bazaar-keepers.

In 1885, although paved, the street contained remnants of its unflattering past. Rue Paul Bert was sometimes regarded as

Hanoi's red-light district. In 1886, a decree was issued to raze the local structures and brothels. Sidewalks with curb and gutter were installed the following year.

In 1888, Rue Paul Bert came into modern being as a street of grandeur. The construction of sophisticated homes and larger, more modern buildings replaced the residual shanty dwellings.

Not to be outdone by Paris, public urinals were constructed on Rue Paul Bert in 1902. In 1914, a small power plant was built near La Petit Lac, producing just enough electricity for the Metropole Hotel and nearby stores.

Shedding its sleazy past, Rue Paul Bert became the most prestigious street in Hanoi.

European shops, their owners living above, provided everything needed including stationery, hardware, dishes, furniture, canned goods, linens, bakery items and other niceties. About thirty-five feet wide, Rue Paul Bert was anchored at the top by the elaborate Hanoi Opera House and, on the opposite corner, by Maison Godard. Farther along Rue Paul Bert, the renowned department store Grands Magasins Reunis, or GMR, provided the latest fashions.

Balconies and sidewalk overhangs shielded shops and cafes from inclement weather. Shoppers could walk freely between stores.

Rue Paul Bert offered the expatriate the same metropolitan distractions as did the boulevards of Paris. One did not have to go far to enjoy fresh croissants and French coffee on a restaurant veranda or a relaxing cigar *pendent l'heure de l'absinthe* in the evenings. Café de la Paix and Café Alexandre were popular venues.

Even with a fashionable *salon parisien de coiffure* frequented by French women as they shopped on Rue Paul Bert, billiard tables were placed in the cafes for the enjoyment of men.

Coming into its own as the business/commercial hub of Hanoi, Rue Paul Bert reveled in its resplendent ascendency. It was the undisputed main street of the capital of Vietnam.

CHAPTER 5

THE A-4 SKYHAWK AND THE F-105 THUNDERCHIEF

The Americans conducted the air war in North Vietnam with the latest aviation technology.

The U.S. Navy used the RA-5C Vigilante and RF-8 for reconnaissance. The coveted F-8 Crusader and the F-4B Phantom II aircraft were indispensable as fighters. The large, twin-engine A-3 Skywarrior served as aerial refueling support. The single engine A-1 Skyraider, a propeller-driven attack plane, was an effective bomber but saw limited use in North Vietnam. Due to its slow speed, the A-1 was more suited to attacks in South Vietnam. The A-6 Intruder, introduced as a day and night bomber, served as a heavy attack plane. The dual-engine Intruder would cause considerable damage to targets in North Vietnam.

The Navy also used the nimble Douglas (later McDonnell-Douglas) A-4 Skyhawk, a single-engine strike bomber, for attacks throughout the Vietnam war.

Ed Heinemann, hailing from Saginaw, Michigan, the designer of the Skyhawk, believed in simplicity and reliability. A self-taught engineer, he excelled with many aircraft designs for the U.S. Navy. When tasked with the design of a jet aircraft to replace the AD Skyraider, Heinemann adhered to his philosophy of efficiency.

Heinemann's A-4, costing less than one million dollars each to manufacture, exceeded Navy specifications. Opting for a design that minimized its size, the heavy mechanism required to fold the wings during carrier operations was eliminated.

Fast, but not supersonic, the A-4 Skyhawk was effective in its attack role. It could carry a wide array of ordnance from five hardpoints under the fuselage and wings. The bomb capacity exceeded that of a World War II B-17 bomber.

In comparison, the U.S. Air Force mobilized a myriad of aircraft including the F-100 Supersabre, F-4C Phantom II, A-1 Skyraider, F-101 Voodoo, the Canberra and B-52 bombers, C-141 and C-130 cargo planes and the small O-1 Birddog, to name a few.

Prior to 1966, the single-engine, supersonic F-105 Thunderchief, the D version being the most prolific, was the workhorse of the U.S. Air Force's tactical bombing campaign.

Designed during the 1950s by Alexander Kartveli, a naturalized American citizen from Georgia, inside the Soviet Union, the F-105, vastly different from the Navy's A-4, was manufactured by Republic Aviation in Farmingdale, New York.

The F-105's primary role dictated a few interesting features: short wings, indented fuselage, hyper-electronics and state-of-the-art advanced avionics.

Originally designed as a slender penetrator of Soviet airspace, the sleek F-105, with an internal weapons bay fifteen feet long accommodating a nuclear bomb—the only single-seat jet with this characteristic—could intrude stealthily into Soviet airspace at low level, climb rapidly to a higher altitude and, with pinpoint precision, release its weapon. The Thunderchief escaped through the sheer speed developed by Pratt and Whitney's powerful J-75 engine that propelled it through the skies at over Mach 2. At sixty-four feet in length, the Thunderchief, famously known for its high speed, outpaced its assailants.

The F-105, affectionately called "Thud," armed with a 20mm Vulcan cannon and air-to-air rockets, also fulfilled the role of a fighter jet. However, it was neither the ideal bomber nor fighter jet for the Vietnam conflict. Still, it shot down thirty MiGs while delivering hundreds of thousands of tons of conventional bombs on targets deep within North Vietnam.

Although the F-105D model carried out the majority of the bombing raids, its losses in Vietnam were excessive. Eight hundred forty F-105s were ultimately manufactured, but of these, about four hundred, almost fifty percent, were shot down.

THE HANOI MARCH

CHAPTER 6

THANH PHO VINH

A Nebraska boy from Seward, Wendell Burke "Wendy" Rivers graduated from high school in 1946. Although too late to participate in World War II, Rivers enlisted in the U.S. Navy. He needed to acquire a college degree if he was to advance in his career. He sought out the Naval Academy and, to his surprise, was appointed to Annapolis from the fleet in 1948. Four years later, he graduated and was commissioned an ensign. Rivers entered flight school in 1953 and earned his wings of gold. He also married his wife with whom he eventually had three children.

On 7 December 1964, the twenty-third anniversary of the Japanese attack on Pearl Harbor, Rivers deployed from Alameda to Vietnam with Attack Squadron VA-155 on the USS *Coral Sea* (CV-43). He began combat missions on the eleventh of February 1965. Seven months later on 10 September, Lieutenant Commander Rivers flew his ninety-sixth combat mission over North Vietnam.

Rivers, strapped into his Skyhawk laden with bombs, felt the acceleration of the catapult as it quickly lunged the A-4 toward the bow of the ship and launched it into the air. Three more Skyhawks followed him. The flight of four assumed a westerly heading over the Gulf of Tonkin toward Thanh Pho (city of) Vinh, just north of Ha Tinh province, directly south of Hanoi.

Spotting the target, a power plant just north of the city, Rivers rolled in from five thousand feet over the grey water. Lining up and descending at a forty-five-degree angle, Rivers and his flight of A-4s initiated their attack.

Wendy Rivers and pilots of the other A-4s, one after another, dropped their bombs and began to pull out of their steep dives. Rivers heard the loud explosions of the bombs as they destroyed the target. Relieved his mission was accomplished successfully, Wendy could "breathe easy." The flight back to his carrier would be smooth.

Then, a loud bang in the rear rocked Wendy's plane. Anti-aircraft artillery, sending multiple shells skyward on a precise trajectory, nailed the A-4.

Rivers immediately turned for the Gulf of Tonkin not far away. He smelled smoke and heard his engine surge wildly. His Skyhawk, trailing flames, totally out of control, went nose down. Rivers pulled the overhead ejection handle and within a quarter second, was instantly propelled out of the cockpit of the doomed Skyhawk.

Once on the ground, Wendy Rivers had no chance to evade capture. He was immediately taken prisoner by the North Vietnamese and, days later, ended up in a dismal, stinking cell in Hanoi.

CHAPTER 7

CHIEN THANG!

The French imposed their dominance throughout colonial Vietnam for many decades, except when the Japanese ruled Indochina during World War II, who, under their guise, allowed a contrived, rogue French organization to administer the territory. After the war and a short interlude with the British and Chiang Kai-shek's Chinese nationalists, a reconstituted France was again in charge of Vietnam, but it wasn't the same.

The upheaval of the war years and the resulting lack of a viable government created a ruling vacuum that spawned an upsurge of Vietnamese discontent. The desire for autonomy was visibly on the rise. The French colonial experiment, under increased assault, became turbulent and tenuous. As a result of a push by occupying Japanese troops just before the end of the war against the loose-knit French, the colonial systems in Vietnam were now in virtual ruin.

Because of complicated British interventions at the war's end and intrigue within the French provisional government, tension between the French and the Vietnamese nationalists escalated. On 19 August 1945, the Viet Minh launched their revolution. Known as the August uprising, it was clear that all of Indochina would become embroiled in savage fighting.

Ho Chi Minh, a chronic smoker, born Nguyen Sinh Cung, rose to lead Vietnam's independence movement.

Combined with his speeches on the steps of the Hanoi Opera House, Ho Chi Minh's independence proclamation in Ba Dinh Square on 2 September 1945 and the battle for Hanoi in December 1946, the Vietnamese cause of self-determination gained momentum.

The Vietnamese military effort to drive out the French became a national cause. Ho Chi Minh was determined to return all of Vietnam to its rightful owner. But there was a tricky catch. As far as Ho Chi Minh was concerned, the rightful owner was not the Vietnamese citizenry, but rather the Communist party.

During the late 1940s and early 1950s, The People's Army of Vietnam, the armed forces of the Viet Minh, itself an abbreviated Vietnamese name for "League for the Independence of Vietnam," under the leadership of General Vo Nguyen Giap, was trying to control northwestern Vietnam and Laos. To counter this threat, the French established a large military base in the flat valley of the Nam Yum River, three hundred kilometers west of Hanoi. That place was called Dien Bien Phu.

Brigadier General Christian de Castries, the commander of French Union forces at Dien Bien Phu, felt his position in the valley was secure. The Viet Minh could not possibly infiltrate enough soldiers to surround and compromise the remote base.

With peripheral supporting strong points, all of which were given female names correlating with the first nine letters of the alphabet, starting with Anne-Marie and ending with Isabelle, the French could control the area. The French, adopting their so-called hedgehog defense, linking the main base with the smaller redoubts, thwarted any concerns of isolation.

Three highways, into and out of the valley, principally from Hanoi or Laos, accessed Dien Bien Phu. Because the French patrolled them daily, General de Castries was confident the stronghold could be supplied overland from Laos; and also, because Dien Bien Phu benefitted from two independent runways, by air from Hanoi. Subsequent events would prove his confidence, based on a lapse in judgment of French logistical capabilities and the wiliness of the Viet Minh, was overreaching.

General Giap, articulate in French and a lover of classical music, took other measures to defeat the colonialists at Dien Bien Phu.

He snaked his army over the mountains and through the valleys, not along the highways.

Day after day, thousands of Viet Minh soldiers walked, marched and crawled their way to the mountains overlooking the Nam Yum valley. They progressed forward through intense rain and ceaseless rough terrain, along paths carved from dense jungles and steep hillsides by tens of thousands of workers.

Artillery components were hand-carried to Dien Bien Phu. Later, the components were reassembled and arrayed on the backside of the mountains (in *defilade* position) northeast of the French encampment.

Giap ranged his big guns with daily bombardments of the French in the valley below. During the night, Viet Minh infantry stealthily descended the slopes of the mountains facing Dien Bien Phu and began digging trenches approaching the French outposts. Face-to-face combat between the French and Viet Minh began in mid-March. Three interlocking northern camps, beginning with Beatrice, fell to the Viet Minh who by now, to the consternation of De Castries, controlled the highways.

Giap deployed his anti-aircraft guns with such effectiveness, he rendered the two French airstrips useless as fighting escalated. Resupply planes could not land. The French, now cut off and isolated, their resources depleted, resorted to parachute drops, but the supplies often fell into the wrong hands.

The Viet Minh excavated miles of interconnected trenches that surrounded the sprawling main French base. Through smaller concentric trenches, tightening the noose, consolidating their presence, the Viet Minh stole closer to the French perimeter.

A ferocious Viet Minh artillery barrage on 1 May 1954 initiated the historic final battle. Several more French outposts of the hedgehog defense fell to the Viet Minh. All through the night of 6 May and during the day of 7 May until three o'clock in the afternoon, the main base was saturated by a focused artillery bombardment from the faraway mountains. As the last of Giap's artillery shells screamed through the air toward the French salient, a large contingent of the Viet Minh army rose from its circumvallation trenches on the valley floor and hammered the main stronghold.

General de Castries surrendered in his underground headquarters. Within seconds, the red Viet Minh flag with a centered yellow star flew over the arched steel roof of his bunker.

The final epic battle was over before dusk. The entire Dien Bien Phu garrison fell to the Viet Minh who kept advancing by the thousands into the base.

The French reign in Indochina came to a quick and bitter end. News of the victory reached Hanoi immediately.

While Jacqueline de Castries, the wife of the Dien Bien Phu French commander, waited anxiously in her room at the Metropole Hotel on Rue Henri Riviere for word about the fate of her husband, Vietnamese celebrated below her balcony. They yelled *Chien Thang*! (Victory!)

The battle of Dien Bien Phu was significant in many ways, not least of which was the demarcation between the Communist Viet Minh in northern Vietnam and those Vietnamese unsupportive of the Communists, mainly Catholics, who moved to southern Vietnam.

The country France once ruled was split in half at the Ben Hai River, at the narrowest part of Vietnam. Tension between the north and the south would increase.

But for now, in the immediate aftermath of Dien Bien Phu, the new Hanoi government, soon to be overwhelmed by emerging administrative and governmental issues, was content for a few days, to celebrate its recent defeat of the French.

Hanoi blossomed. Colorful flowers hung from balconies as vibrant red and yellow bunting cascaded down the buildings' streetside facades. Red flags of the new Communist government, waving throughout the city, were prolific. The plaza in front of the Hanoi Opera House was packed for days with ecstatic people.

The Vietnamese civilian population gathered by the tens of thousands to welcome home its glorious soldiers as they marched victoriously in a parade on Rue Paul Bert, Hanoi's famed, elegant main avenue.

CHAPTER 8

CAUGHT BY GROUNDFIRE NEAR THANH HOA

Born in 1933, Render Crayton was a native of Charlotte, North Carolina. He enrolled in the Navy Reserve Officer Training Corps (NROTC) at Georgia Tech University. Upon graduation in June 1954, a month after the debacle of Dien Bien Phu, Crayton received his commission as an ensign. In August 1955, Crayton was awarded his wings as a naval aviator.

Initially assigned to VA-175, a Navy attack squadron in Jacksonville, Florida, he flew the AD-5 Skyraider until 1957. This was followed with an assignment as a pilot to the Naval Air Reserve training unit at Norfolk, Virginia from December 1957 until November 1959.

Crayton's aviation career continued at Corpus Christi and Kingsville Naval Air Stations for all of 1960 and 1961. He was an instructor pilot on the Grumman Cougar jet which replaced the Panther jet.

Crayton served on board a carrier as an aviation fuels officer for two years until November 1963. From there, he transitioned to the A-4 Skyhawk through a training program with the Replacement Air Group (RAG) at Lemoore, California for seven months to June 1964. Crayton was then assigned to attack squadron VA-56, also stationed at Lemoore Naval Air Station.

Lieutenant Commander Crayton made two deployments with VA-56 to the Gulf of Tonkin aboard the USS *Ticonderoga* (CV-14). He flew combat missions from July to November 1964 and, for a second time, starting in November 1965.

On 7 February 1966, Crayton's A-4 Skyhawk, flying near Thanh Hoa on armed reconnaissance, was caught by groundfire while attacking a convoy of trucks. Engulfed in an exploding fireball, Crayton ejected and parachuted to earth. Throughout the ordeal, Crayton's radio communications were calm and composed. Knowing the A-4s in his flight circling overhead were nearing a low fuel state, Crayton told them to depart. Rescue helicopters, damaged by ground fire, could not pick him up.

Crayton was hauled off by North Vietnamese militia. At thirty-two years old, Render Crayton became a prisoner in Hanoi.

CHAPTER 9

INDEPENDENCE AND CHANGE

After the Viet Minh victory at Dien Bien Phu, all French place names in Hanoi were changed to reflect Vietnamese preferences. La Grand Lac became Tay Ho and La Petit Lac became Hoan Kiem Ho.

Street names were changed as well. Rue Henri Riviere on which sat the famous Metropole Hotel, now Kach San Hoa Binh, became Pho Ngo Quyen. Three of the four broad, parallel streets, Boulevards Rollandes, Carreau, and Gambetta became respectively, Pho Hai Ba Trung, Pho Ly Thuong Kiet and Pho Tran Hung Dao.

Rue Paul Bert, the fourth parallel street down which victorious Viet Minh soldiers marched in triumph after Dien Bien Phu, became Pho Trang Tien. A derivative of two characters in ancient Nom Script, Trang Tien does not lend itself well to a literal translation. Loosely, the name means "money area" or "coinage forge."

The most popular street in Hanoi, regardless of name, Pho Trang Tien still constituted the principal thoroughfare, the main shopping boulevard, the street on which breathed the life of Hanoi. The long street was further subdivided into three additional names: Pho Hang Khay, Pho Trang Thi and Pho Nguyen Thai Hoc, respectively. Contrasting with Pho Trang Tien, these three streets were shaded by enormous Xa Cu and Muom mahogany trees.

Neither the Democratic (Socialist) Republic of Vietnam nor the Republic of Vietnam, respectively north and south of the demilitarized zone (DMZ), ever really knew peace after 1954. While the countryside, controlled by the Viet Minh, was dangerous, Hanoi and other urban centers, were, for the most part, safe.

But then, less than a decade after the Viet Minh victory and Vietnamese independence, *Nguoi My*, the Americans, came from across the Pacific Ocean.

The conflict between North Vietnam and America began in the early 1960s and boiled over into war in 1964 with America's Gulf of Tonkin Resolution. On 7 August 1964, the scant three hundred fifty-word document passed quickly through the United States Congress. Obtuse in its wording, the resolution granted the American president his ticket to war, giving him virtually unlimited war-making powers. Everett Alvarez, captured at Hon Gay, experienced the beginning firsthand.

To American airmen, Hanoi was no more tangible than names on an old map, a place of mild mystery. Never did an American airman from bases in Thailand or from aircraft carriers in the Gulf of Tonkin, what the Vietnamese referred to as Vinh Bac Bo (Northern Sea), think he would become a permanent fixture in North Vietnam's capital city.

The Viet Minh held a victory celebration of Dien Bien Phu in 1954 on Hanoi's Rue Paul Bert. Twelve years later on 6 July 1966, the same avenue, now called Pho Trang Tien, inadvertently stepped into history in another fitful way, but the circumstances were different.

CHAPTER 10

SOUTHWEST OF DONG HOI

Born in Cleveland, Ohio in 1933, Alan Lurie graduated from high school and enrolled in Ohio State University from where in 1955 he earned a degree and an officer's commission in the United States Air Force. He was called to active duty, proceeded through flight training and was proudly awarded his hard-earned wings. He eventually transitioned to the F-4C Phantom II as aircraft commander. Alan Lurie and his wife had two daughters and a son.

On the first of February 1966, Captain Lurie, along with First Lieutenant Darrel Pyle with the 480th Tactical Fighter Squadron, deployed to Da Nang from where they undertook combat missions throughout North Vietnam.

On 13 June 1966, a flight of Phantoms of the 480th TFS departed Da Nang airbase and headed due north. Captain Lurie, the pilot, and Lieutenant Pyle, the Pilot/Systems Officer (PSO), later designated as Weapons System Officer (WSO), in the Phantom's backseat, were among them. The flight was conducting armed reconnaissance near Dong Hoi, in the southern reaches of North Vietnam, just north of the DMZ.

The flight followed Highway One which was continuously interdicted by the Americans from the air, especially in the southern part of North Vietnam.

Southwest of Dong Hoi, the flight attacked a target. Captain Lurie's aircraft was damaged by multiple anti-aircraft fire. Flying at almost five hundred miles per hour, Lurie ejected three hundred feet above the ground. He felt the blast of air on his face even though he had drawn down the face curtain. His helmet was almost ripped from his head. The rapid ejection injured Lurie's spine.

Captain Lurie, recovering from his parachute drop, now on the ground and in acute pain, slowly stood upright only to face hundreds of rifle muzzles. Immediately captured, Lurie was tied up.

Born on 25 April 1940, Darrel Pyle, from Compton, California, in the F-4's backseat, ejected prior to Lurie and was taken prisoner separately.

Together for the next several days, the two Americans, deprived of food and water, and suffering brutal beatings, were put on display as they were taken to Hanoi, arriving there on 29 June 1966.

CHAPTER 11

PHAO PHONG KHONG

During their involvement in North Vietnam, American pilots fell prey to ground-based anti-aircraft defenses manned by determined North Vietnamese forces.

At the most rudimentary level, soldiers learned to shoot rifles at small model airplane targets pulled along ziplines that simulated the flight of real aircraft.

Crews of as many as eight persons, coalescing into expert teams, trained together on heavy anti-aircraft artillery in the hinterlands of remote Hoa Binh Province. Recruits studied operational specifications, range, declination, various fuses and explosive warheads. They read handbooks and manuals depicting the silhouettes of U.S. planes. They learned how to operate and maintain various large caliber guns.

Some of the best air defense artillerists, using weapons ranging from basic single shot carbines to complex 120mm anti-aircraft artillery, were females. As Ho Chi Minh stressed, women also have to fight alongside the men.

The Russian-made ZPU-4, a heavy, quad-barrel machine gun with a total combined maximum rate of fire of two thousand four hundred rounds per minute, was a potent weapon. Operating the gun effectively required significant training.

More powerful, the 57mm and smaller 37mm Phao Phong

Khong, anti-aircraft artillery, Triple-A (AAA), as the Americans termed it, augmented North Vietnam's air defense capabilities. Precisely manufactured, the weapons were imported from Russia and China. While the 57mm gun was loaded mechanically from a tray on the side, the smaller caliber 37mm weapon was loaded by hand from the top, a cumbersome technique.

Feeding an armed clip of five rounds, each clip weighing a little more than fifteen pounds, into the gun's top breach required careful timing. Through continuous loading, clip-by-clip, the M1939 gun could fire one hundred sixty rounds per minute. Each 37mm projectile had an effective altitude of thirteen thousand feet.

As potent as North Vietnam's anti-aircraft artillery was in 1964, they had at its disposal only one thousand five hundred anti-aircraft guns.

During his visit to Hanoi on 6 February 1965, Russian Premier Alexei Nikolayevich Kosygin agreed to provide Hanoi with additional anti-aircraft artillery, a most desirous gift. By 1966, the number of anti-aircraft guns, of which over one thousand were radar-controlled, totaled more than six thousand.

The North Vietnamese wanted more. They pressed Russia for surface-to-air missiles, or SAMs, as they came to be called. The request was granted. Vietnamese crews, backed and trained by Russian counterparts, became adroit with the operations of the SA-2 and later the more sophisticated, more robust SA-3 surface-to-air missiles.

In early April 1965, U.S. reconnaissance flights over North Vietnam made an alarming discovery. Even though the President of the United States declared a twenty-five-mile radius bombing exclusion zone around Hanoi and Haiphong, SAMs were being installed not far from Hanoi.

Anti-aircraft artillery sites and SAM installations eventually ringed the metropolitan areas. The two cities came to have the world's most formidable anti-aircraft defense system. Not static, North Vietnam's air defenses were moved and relocated often.

While North Vietnam was not particularly sophisticated in terms of industrial output, its strategic anti-aircraft gun and missile deployments, thousands of miles of civilian trenches, and many thousands of bomb shelters of all sizes proved effective.

North Vietnamese gunners reveled in confrontations with American pilots. When word came back that a gun or missile crew shot down an American aircraft, the gunners were jubilant. The triumphant Dien Bien Phu cry rang out again: *Chien Thang*!

A better trophy than the downing of an American plane could not be imagined. The victory was sweeter when a gun crew learned the pilot, dressed in his flight suit and helmet, had been captured alive—*Welcome to the Socialist Republic of Vietnam*!

THE HANOI MARCH

CHAPTER 12

DISASTER AT KEP

C ole Black was born in 1932 near Lake City, Minnesota on Lake
Pepin, a large pool on the Mississippi River southeast of Min-
neapolis. He grew up on a rural farm and attended a country grade
school. During his high school years, he took a keen interest in
sports and came to appreciate the competitiveness of football and
wrestling. He joined the Navy at age seventeen and, for his first
five years, served as an electronic technician.

Cole Black earned his commission at Officer Candidate School
in Newport, Rhode Island. Black was also awarded his Navy wings
in 1957 and flew as a reconnaissance pilot. He went on to receive
his B.S. degree from Monterey Naval Post Graduate School.

Rotating through several flying assignments, Cole Black eventually flew combat missions in Vietnam.

Having completed one combat cruise and shy by seven days of
completing his second, Lieutenant Commander Black, the Execu-
tive Officer of Fighter Squadron VF-211, piloting an F-8 Crusader,
along with other Crusaders, took off from the USS *Hancock* (CVA-
19), ninety miles off the shore of North Vietnam on 21 June 1966.

Black's flight escorted Crusader photo-reconnaissance planes
designated as RF-8As with squadron VFP-63. The photo-reconnaissance Crusaders and their F-8 escorts, entered Vietnam airspace
north of Hai Phong and headed toward Kep, northeast of Hanoi.

Lieutenant Leonard Eastman, on his forty-fifth reconnaissance mission, piloted one of the RF-8As.

Born in 1933, Eastman hailed from Bernardston, Massachusetts. He graduated from Northeastern University in Boston in 1957 and immediately joined the Navy to become a naval aviator. After flight training, Eastman became expert in photo reconnaissance.

Now, on 21 June 1966, near Lang Son, North Vietnam, not far from Kep, Lieutenant Eastman met with trouble.

Eastman's plane, flying at four thousand feet altitude at five hundred knots, was struck by anti-aircraft fire along the rail line to China. The RF-8, engulfed in flames, fell out of control. Eastman immediately ejected from his aircraft.

Cole Black and his flight of four F-8s were diverted from their escort mission of other reconnaissance aircraft to establish support for the rescue attempt of Lieutenant Eastman. Black, knowing the rescue effort could be prolonged, sent two Crusaders to refuel from a tanker while he and his wingman orbited the area where Eastman was last seen. Unknown to them, Eastman had been captured.

Cole Black and his wingman saw four MiGs approaching fast. The MiG pilots apparently did not see the F-8s. Black maneuvered behind them but as he did, he ventured too close to an anti-aircraft artillery site. Triple-A fire from 57mm guns opened up. A series of explosions occurred around him, rocking the aircraft. Shrapnel ripped through the long fuselage of Cole Black's F-8 disabling the plane's hydraulic systems.

"I'm hit," Black called out to his wingman.

One of the MiGs fired at Black but missed.

Black's F-8 lost its primary hydraulic system. He fought for control and began a turn to the east. His wingman was close by.

With limited control and knowing the plane's hydraulics would fail quickly, Cole Black tried to make the safety of the Gulf of Tonkin where a U.S. rescue helicopter could fish him from the water. But like Harry Brubaker in James Michener's *Bridges at Toko-Ri*, the odds were not in his favor.

Black's Crusader pitched down and headed straight for the earth. Cole Black, the farm kid from Minnesota, initiated the seat ejection system but lost his hold on the face curtain which interrupted the firing sequence. The ejection seat didn't activate. With only seconds remaining, Black yanked the face curtain which set off a loud explosion. He was shot out of his Crusader near Kep airfield.

His parachute collapsing next to him, Black hit the ground and rolled. The air was knocked from his lungs. He was immediately surrounded by village people.

Black was surprised by how well he was treated. While no one smiled, not at him anyway, the Vietnamese didn't harm him either. That all changed when he was transferred to the militia. His treatment went from benign to bad, then very bad.

Handcuffed and blindfolded, Black was thrown into a truck. He was bound for Hanoi. Put on frequent display for local citizens along the way, Black's road trip was punctuated by frequent stops. Many villagers stared at Black out of curiosity, but others were extremely hostile and accosted him repeatedly.

Black, never freed from his restraining bindings, finally arrived in Hanoi. Instead of facilitating Leonard Eastman's rescue, Cole Black joined him in captivity.

THE HANOI MARCH

CHAPTER 13

HANOI'S PRISONS AND THE RABBIT

Hoa Lo prison was built by the French in Hanoi in the 1880s. Dubbed the "Hanoi Hilton" by a future prisoner named Robert "Bob" Shumaker, Hoa Lo, an imposing, morbid facility, served as the primary receiving center of captured American airmen. The perimeter stone wall, fifteen feet high and two-feet thick, outlining an oddly-shaped trapezoid, completely occupied three acres in the downtown area. The prison facility was bound on all sides by city streets. The frontal wall dominated one side of Hoa Lo Street, so named for small furnaces (Hoa Lo) once fabricated by street merchants in the immediate vicinity. The words Maison Centrale were inscribed on the arch above the prison's only entrance.

Filthy cells held prisoners in isolation, in twos and in groups as large as forty. Prisoners were shackled in leg irons secured to concrete slabs which served as beds.

Americans, held separately from Vietnamese inmates, gave each section of "the Hilton" a colorful name contrasting with the horror that took place there. Names such as Heartbreak, New Guy Village and Las Vegas became infamous.

However, Hanoi's Maison Centrale was not constructed to hold

American military prisoners. Each day, as the number of captured Americans grew, the prison system became strained. The Hanoi government was obliged to find a solution for the number of enemy airmen who increasingly fell into their hands.

In addition to Hoa Lo, starting in 1965, Americans were held in two additional locations around Hanoi.

On the southwest periphery of the city, Nga Tu So, an old movie studio, was converted into a prison specifically for American prisoners in August-September 1965. The makeshift prison consisted of one gate and ten buildings. The Americans referred to the facility at first as Camp America, then later, because the cells allowed guards to watch them like caged animals, the Zoo. The Americans gave each prison building its own name: Pigsty, Garage, Barn, Pool Hall, Library and Quiz Room.

Thirty-three miles to the northwest of Hanoi, the North Vietnamese opened a special compound in August 1965. Built in a square from concrete blocks, stone and brick, the prison contained nine unconnected buildings each holding as many as eight prisoners, two to a room in cells seven feet by nine feet. Each cell, without light for most of the day, contained two wood plank beds and a small barred air opening to the outside. Temperatures in the buildings, which sat on the east side of a hill, became unbearably hot in summer and freezing cold in winter. The Vietnamese called the facility *Xom Ap Lo* or *Bat Bat*. The Americans named it Tic-Tac-Toe camp due to its regular grid shape. The prison, noted for its remoteness, was given other names—Farm and Country Club—but ultimately became more derisively referred to as Briar Patch.

Notorious for deprivation, austere and grim to the extreme, the environment of each Vietnam prison facility was appallingly stark. The American prisoners had nothing: no electricity and little sunlight, no circulating air and very little clean water. Food, when and if it was served, provided meager nourishment. Diarrhea and dysentery were rampant. Medical attention was denied. Days were long, idleness and cramped cells the norm. Communication with the outside world was nil. Brutality and harassment were constant, the possibility of escape eliminated. As a result, some airmen fell into deep depression.

To newly arrived American captives, Vietnamese officials and guards looked the same. Only after time, did the features or characteristics of each person with whom the Americans dealt begin to stand out. Never knowing their real names, the Americans referred to them sarcastically by distinguishing traits, prominent physical features or mannerisms.

Some comically-descriptive nicknames, which were numerous, included Spot, due to a white blemish on his face, Mickey Mouse, Rat, Lump, Elf, Frenchy, Groucho, Dog and Fox.

One Vietnamese figured prominently in the North Vietnamese-American prisoner relationship.

* * * *

Nguyen Minh Y was born in 1940. His father, a doctor, gave his son the name "Y," (pronounced *Eeee*), a stand-alone letter-name meaning medicine.* Y entered college in 1960, but before he completed his education was drafted into the North Vietnamese army. Y spoke several languages, English and Russian being two of them. Although relatively proficient with English—Y thought highly of his linguistic skills—he often made amusing pronunciation and grammatical mistakes. He spoke in a regional dialect common to the central part of Vietnam which, when Y was excited or irritated, sometimes caused him to pronounce an S as an Sh.

Y received a commission as a *thieu uy* (second lieutenant) in 1964-65. He was assigned to the Enemy Proselytizing Department.

Y was at the forefront of communications with and the questioning of American airmen taken captive. He served as chief interrogator-interpreter, organizer and contact point for gaining

---

*Word order for Vietnamese names is surname first, middle name, given name.

information from the Americans. Y visited the prisons frequently and escorted a few downed American airmen captured in the countryside to Hanoi.

Nguyen Minh Y enjoyed watching each American suffer. He was convinced that each "creemeenal" would break sooner or later.

Because of his impish grin, slightly buck teeth and large protruding ears, the Americans gave Nguyen Minh Y a funny nickname. They called him the Rabbit.

CHAPTER 14

OTHERS WHO MADE THE CUT

On 6 July 1966, half of the one hundred Americans shot down and captured to date in North Vietnam were singled out. They made the cut, however ironic that expression may be, for something unknown. Everett Alvarez, the first American to be shot down, was included.

The second American airman to be captured in North Vietnam was Navy pilot Bob Shumaker. Between the shootdown of Everett Alvarez and six months later that of Shumaker, more than thirty pilots were killed in the skies over North Vietnam.

Lieutenant Commander Shumaker, born in New Castle, Pennsylvania in 1933, flew the F-8 Crusader with fighter squadron VF-154 off the USS *Coral Sea*. His plane was struck by anti-aircraft fire on 11 February 1965 over the south of North Vietnam.

Shumaker, steadying an erratic plane, keyed his mic announcing the side number of his plane and that he was in trouble.

"Four oh three . . ."

He wasn't able to finish his statement before he had to eject.

Shumaker's parachute opened less than fifty feet above ground. Injured with a broken back, Shumaker was captured, brutally beaten and transported to Hanoi.

* * * *

On 2 March 1965, First Lieutenant Hayden Lockhart, born on 16 June 1938 in Cambridge, Massachusetts, participated in the first Rolling Thunder strike.

Lockhart, flying an F-100 with the 613th Tactical Fighter Squadron from Da Nang, was providing flak suppression for a main strike on an ammunition dump near Xom Bang, seven miles north of the DMZ when he was hit. He ejected and evaded capture for over a week until surrounded.

* * * *

On 20 April 1965, during a night mission south of Thanh Hoa, Lieutenant Commander Phillip Butler spotted trucks on the highway. Flying an A-4C with attack squadron VA-22 from the USS *Midway* (CV-41), Butler rolled in and dropped his bombs. They detonated immediately below his aircraft and blew its wings off. Butler, a native of Tulsa, Oklahoma, born in 1938, a graduate of the U.S. Naval Academy, ejected near Vinh. Once on the ground, Butler evaded capture until caught by North Vietnamese using German Shepherd search dogs.

* * * *

Air Force Captain Ronald Storz, a thirty-three-year-old native of South Ozone Park, Long Island, flew the O-1 Birddog spotter plane, a modified single-engine, high-wing Cessna aircraft. On 28 April 1965, Storz flew from Hue-Phu Bai to the Ben Hai River which marked the DMZ, the separation between South and North Vietnam. His aircraft went down on the north side of the river and he was captured. Storz's survival gun was taken, cocked and pointed at his head while he was forced to kneel on the ground. Storz knew he was a dead man, but the trigger was never pulled. Storz was tied up and taken north to Hanoi, a ten-day trip.

* * * *

Captain Robert Peel flew the F-105 with the 333rd Tactical Fighter Squadron from Takhli, Thailand. Born in Memphis, Tennessee in 1939, Peel was shot down on 31 May 1965 while on a bombing mission against the Ham Rong Bridge. He ejected and was captured south of Thanh Hoa.

* * * *

Flying with VA-23 off the USS *Midway* on 2 June 1965, Lieutenant John "JB" McKamey's A-4E Skyhawk sustained ground fire over the Song Ca (Ca River) near Vinh. The thirty-year-old McKamey, from Greencastle, Indiana, ejected. Minutes later, he was overwhelmed by the North Vietnamese.

* * * *

U.S. Air Force Major Lawrence "Larry" Guarino flew the famous British Spitfire in Italy and North Africa before America entered World War II. He eventually piloted the P-51 Mustang and the F-86 Sabre in Korea.

On the fourteenth of June 1965, Major Guarino, a New Jersey boy, forty-four years of age, flying an F-105D from Korat with the 44th Tactical Fighter Squadron, was shot down. He landed in the countryside and was immediately surrounded by villagers.

* * * *

Captain Paul Kari, a 1958 graduate of Ohio State University, had the dubious honor of flying the first F-4 Phantom II to be shot down during the Vietnam War. Kari was flying with the 45th Tactical Fighter Squadron from Ubon airbase. On the twentieth of June 1965, over the target near Son La, the ceiling being only three thousand feet, Kari's F-4 was damaged when anti-aircraft fire struck his Phantom during his bombing run. He and his backseater Curt Briggs ejected. Briggs was eventually rescued. Captain Kari, however, caught and tied up, was on his way to Hanoi.

* * * *

An Alabama native, born in 1924, Commander Jeremiah Denton, with attack squadron VA-75, piloted an A-6 Intruder. Denton and his Bombardier/Navigator (BN), Lieutenant (j.g.) William Tschudy, from Illinois, born in 1935, flew from the deck of the USS *Independence* (CV-62), an Atlantic-based carrier on its only tour in the Gulf of Tonkin. On a mission to destroy the port in Thanh Hoa on July 18, 1965, they launched from their carrier the same day Secretary of Defense Robert McNamara visited the ship.

What plagued Phil Butler three months before occurred again. A bomb prematurely exploded beneath Denton's plane. Denton and Tschudy ejected and were captured near the target.

* * * *

On 24 July 1965, Captain Richard "Pop" Keirn, born in Akron, Ohio, in 1924, a prisoner in Germany during World War II, flew his F-4 with the 47th Tactical Fighter Squadron from Ubon while covering a formation of F-105s on a mission at Lang Chi. Keirn was forced to eject into the hands of the North Vietnamese after an explosion of a Russian SA-2 missile damaged his plane. His was the first downing of an American plane in Vietnam by a surface-to-air missile. His backseater was killed.

* * * *

Captain Kile "Red" Berg, born in Redlands, California, in 1939, flew an F-105 with the 563rd Tactical Fighter Squadron based at Takhli. On 27 July 1965, because of Keirn's incident, Berg and a force of fifty aircraft were sent for the first time to attack the missile sites near Hanoi. Struck by ground fire, ejecting, then captured, Berg was soon headed to Hoa Lo.

Due to a deaf sister, Kile Berg learned how to communicate using his fingers. He taught his fellow prisoners the American finger spelling system, augmenting the tap code brought by Smitty Harris.

On the same raid as Berg, Captain Robert Purcell, known as

Percy, an F-105 pilot born on 14 February 1931 in Louisville, Kentucky, now with the 12th Tactical Fighter Squadron, was also shot down and captured.

* * * *

Richard "Skip" Brunhaver, from Washington state, age twenty-five, an A-4 pilot with attack squadron VA-22, launched from *Midway* before dusk on 24 August 1965. After attacking a bridge south of Thanh Hoa, Brunhaver attempted to pull his Skyhawk out of its dive when he realized he had a mechanical malfunction. Unable to effectively climb, the plane glanced off a jagged ridge. Brunhaver ejected from his crippled A-4. He survived the parachute descent but fell into the hands of the North Vietnamese.

* * * *

In a separate incident on 24 August 1965, Lieutenant Commander Robert Doremus, an F-4B Radio Intercept Officer (RIO) with fighter squadron VF-21 off *Midway* was downed by a SAM near the Ham Rong Bridge. Doremus, a native of Montclair, New Jersey, became a prisoner of the North Vietnamese along with the pilot.

* * * *

On 26 August 1965, Lieutenant (j.g.) Edward Davis, from Philadelphia, Pennsylvania, flew his fifty-seventh mission in a propeller-driven A-1 Skyraider with attack squadron VA-152 off the USS *Oriskany* (CV-34). Davis, his plane damaged by ground fire just north of the DMZ, unbuckled his harness and moved the canopy aft. The A-1 flipped down throwing Davis out of the cockpit. He found the D-ring to his parachute and pulled it. Once on the ground, Davis was overwhelmed by North Vietnamese militia.

* * * *

A few weeks later, on 5 October 1965, Bruce Seeber, from Lowpoint, Illinois, an Air Force captain on temporary duty with the 49th

Tactical Fighter Squadron at Takhli, was on a mission in an F-105 to bomb the Lang Met bridge located twenty miles south of the Chinese border. Seeber was shot down and soon on his way to Hanoi.

* * * *

First Lieutenant Tom Barrett, from Lombard, Illinois, born in 1939, was the Pilot/Systems Officer in an F-4C, on temporary duty with the 43th Tactical Fighter Squadron at Ubon airbase. Barrett was flying with Captain James Hivner, the pilot, who was born in 1931 in Elizabethtown, Illinois when also on 5 October 1965, the same day as Seeber, their plane was shot down thirty miles northeast of Hanoi. Both men, now captives, were taken to Hoa Lo in the back of a dump truck along with parts of their aircraft.

* * * *

Lieutenant Commander James Bell, from Ohio, born on 29 April 1931, piloted an RA-5C Vigilante with squadron RVAH-1 off USS *Independence*. He and James "Duffy" Hutton, an ex-school teacher from Washington, D.C., age thirty-five, now the Vigilante's Radio Intercept Officer (RIO), went looking for missile sites east of Haiphong on 16 October 1965. Their Vigilante was immediately targeted by anti-aircraft artillery gunners. Small, but deadly warheads tore through the plane. Both aviators ejected. Pulled from the sea by North Vietnamese fishermen, Bell, his left shoulder injured, and Hutton ended up in Hanoi.

* * * *

On the seventeenth of October, Lieutenant (j.g.) Porter Halyburton, born in Miami, Florida in 1941, flying with VF-84, also off the *Independence*, was providing flak suppression in support of a strike force north of Hanoi. His F-4 Phantom sustained a direct hit. Halyburton pulled the ejection D-ring lanyard. He shot out of the F-4's back cockpit and parachuted to earth into the hands of the North Vietnamese. The Phantom's pilot was killed.

* * * *

Lieutenant (j.g.) Ralph Gaither, born in Birmingham, Alabama, on 8 March 1942, was the pilot in another F-4B Phantom also with VF-84 on the same mission on 17 October 1965. Gaither's F-4 was shot down after the raid. He and Lieutenant (j.g.) Rodney Knutson, the RIO, ejected just south of the Chinese border. They were taken to Hoa Lo.

* * * *

First Lieutenant Edward Alan Brudno, born in 1940 in Quincy, Massachusetts, flew as a Pilot/Systems Officer in an F-4C with the 68th Tactical Fighter Squadron based at Korat airbase. On 18 October 1965, a raid was initiated against a railway bridge near the town of Ha Tinh. The Phantom encountered Triple-A fire. Forced to eject, Brudno was captured and transported to Hanoi.

* * * *

On 5 November 1965, an A-1E based at Udorn was downed while flying a search and rescue mission. The next day, November sixth, a CH-3C helicopter with call sign "Jolly Green 85" of the 48th Air Rescue Squadron also based in Udorn, Thailand, made a rescue attempt of the downed A-1 pilot.

Near the rescue site, Jolly Green 85, taking heavy small arms fire, was doomed to crash. The pilot gained enough altitude for the entire crew to bail out. Arthur Cormier, a thirty-two-year-old West Orange, New Jersey boy and Jerry Singleton, born in 1940 in Oklahoma City, and Bob Lilly, all with para-rescue squadron ARRS-38, became prisoners.

* * * *

Captain Jon Reynolds from Philadelphia, born in 1937, flew with the 335th Tactical Fighter Squadron from Takhli. On November 28, 1965, he was on a mission in an F-105 near Van Yen, west of

Hanoi. Riddled by automatic ground fire, he nursed his Thunderchief ten miles to the south before he ejected. Not long after, bound and blindfolded, Reynolds was escorted to Hanoi.

* * * *

Marine Corps Major Howard "Howie" Dunn, a Montana native, age thirty-five, conducted a night escort mission on 7 December 1965, west of Thanh Hoa. Dunn's F-4, with VMF/A 323 was badly damaged by the explosion of a SA-2 surface-to-air missile. Howie Dunn, who had no option but to eject, evaded capture. On the sixth day, he was overwhelmed by the North Vietnamese. John Frederick, Dunn's RIO, was also captured but died later.

* * * *

On 23 December 1965, twenty-seven-year-old Lieutenant (j.g.) William Shankel from San Andreas, California, flying with VA-94 off the USS *Enterprise* (CVN-65) was in a flight of A-4s when, at the bottom of his bombing dive against the Hai Duong Bridge, the A-4 was struck by anti-aircraft fire. Shankel ejected not far from the target. He tore his knee which immobilized him. Shankel was soon hauled off to prison.

* * * *

Lieutenant Gerald "Jerry" Coffee, born on 2 June 1934 in Modesto, California, was awarded his Navy wings in 1959. Seven years later, Lieutenant Coffee flew the RA-5C Vigilante with RVAH-13 from the deck of the USS *Kitty Hawk* (CV-63). On the third of February 1966, just hours before *Kitty Hawk* would rotate off its line duty, Coffee, with Robert Hanson sitting in the backseat, launched for a road reconnaissance mission north of Vinh. After completion of the mission, just as they turned east toward *Kitty Hawk*, their plane was shredded by anti-aircraft fire. Coffee ejected immediately after Bob Hansen. Coffee, now captured by the North Vietnamese, believed Hanson was also captured.

Jerry Coffee was gagged and shoved against a tree behind which his hands were tied. His shoulder, broken during the ejection, sent acute pain through his body. Coffee was being treated to a mock firing squad that wasn't so mock. A teenage soldier failed to unload a chambered round and the en-bloc clip from his M-1 rifle. While firing pins in rifles other than his clicked harmlessly when the order to fire was given, the unwitting soldier squeezed off the round. The 30-06 bullet splintered the tree next to Coffee's head.

That evening, while *Kitty Hawk* was sailing south to the bright lights of Hong Kong for two weeks of R and R, Jerry Coffee was headed to Hanoi.

* * * *

On 18 February 1966, Lieutenant (j.g.) Larry Spencer, born on 12 May 1940, hailing from West Des Moines, Iowa, was flying as a RIO in an F-4B with VA-92 off the USS *Enterprise*. His Phantom was hit by a surface-to-air missile near Thanh Hoa. Spencer ejected and immediately lost consciousness. When he came to, he was dangling beneath his parachute over the Gulf of Tonkin. A Parsons College graduate, Spencer was fished from the sea by the North Vietnamese and transported to prison. The pilot was killed.

* * * *

Lieutenant (j.g.) James Greenwood, the pilot, and Lieutenant (j.g.) Richard Ratzlaff, the aircraft RIO, both in the same F-4B also with VF-92, launched from *Enterprise* on 20 March 1966. They attacked a bridge southwest of Vinh during which the Phantom was damaged. The two aviators ejected just off the coast. While Greenwood was rescued by a Navy helicopter, Ratzlaff, not quite twenty-four, from Aberdeen, South Dakota, now in the water, had no chance of escape.

* * * *

Arthur Burer, born in 1932 in San Antonio, Texas, stationed at Udorn airbase, was on a mission on 21 March 1966 in his twin-engine RF-101C Voodoo aircraft of the 45th Tactical Reconnaissance Squadron. Over Hon Me Island, near the coast of North Vietnam, ground fire smashed into Captain Burer's plane. Burer ejected. The Vietnamese caught up with him when he reached the ground.

* * * *

Captain Charles "Chuck" Boyd, a native of Rockwell City, Iowa, born in 1938, went to Korat airbase in November 1965 as an F-105 pilot with the 421st Tactical Fighter Squadron. In mid-February 1966, Boyd was on a flight in northeast Laos when his plane's machine-gun exploded. His F-105's engine ingested gun parts and Boyd was forced to eject. He was rescued.

Later, on 22 April 1966, flying northwest of Hanoi, Captain Boyd attacked a SAM site just outside Hanoi. His plane sustained multiple strikes from heavy ground fire. Boyd ejected again. Once on the ground, Boyd, not as fortunate as the first time, was overwhelmed by North Vietnamese ground troops and hauled to prison.

* * * *

Air Force Major Alan Brunstrom grew up in South Dakota and Missouri. He joined the Air Force at age seventeen. Years later, Brunstrom, thirty-five years old, now with a wife and daughter, reported for duty in March 1966 with the 20th Tactical Reconnaissance Squadron in Udorn, Thailand. On 22 April, Brunstrom flew photo reconnaissance in the RF-101C Voodoo aircraft fifty miles northeast of Hanoi. Struck by groundfire, Brunstrom ejected. He landed in the soft mud of a rice patty and was quickly surrounded by enemy forces.

* * * *

A member of the 469th Tactical Fighter Squadron, flying an F-105 from Korat airbase, First Lieutenant Jerry Driscoll, on his bombing run to destroy the Phu Lang Thuong Bridge northeast of

Hanoi, met with anti-aircraft ground fire on 24 April 1966. Driscoll, ejected. Covered with lacerations, he parachuted to earth only to meet the same fate as others before him. Jerry Driscoll, aged twenty-six from Chicago, became a prisoner in North Vietnam.

* * * *

Captain David Hatcher, a North Carolinian born in 1934, flew an F-105 with the 333rd Tactical Fighter Squadron based at Takhli. On his second strafing run against a rail line west of Hanoi on 30 May 1966, Hatcher's plane was struck. Forced to eject, he was soon cornered by the North Vietnamese.

* * * *

Navy Lieutenant Paul Galanti, from Lodi, New Jersey, grew up in an Army family, but attended the Naval Academy. Born in 1939, Galanti earned his Navy wings in 1962.

Galanti was assigned to VA-216 as an A-4C pilot on board the USS *Hancock*. On his ninety-seventh combat mission while attacking a railroad siding near Vinh on 17 June 1966, his A-4 was struck by ground fire. Paul Galanti, age twenty-seven, was forced to eject. He joined other American prisoners at Hoa Lo. Galanti's picture, taken later in Hanoi, would appear on the cover of *Life Magazine* in 1967. He was wearing drab prison clothes.

THE HANOI MARCH

PART TWO

THE GATHERING

THE HANOI MARCH

CHAPTER 15

THE GET-OUT-OF-BED GONG

At 4:30 a.m., in the pre-dawn of 6 July 1966, small lanterns softly illuminated the dark maze of nooks and narrow pathways that characterized Hanoi's neighborhoods. The streets of Hoan Kiem District were empty. Concealed in isolated enclaves, damp laundry hung limply from windows and clotheslines that were strung between adjacent buildings.

Two old women tended a small wood fire on a narrow sidewalk just off Hai Ba Trung Street. Wispy steam rose from large, round metal pots as the women, working by candlelight, chopped up chickens to be thrown into boiling water for breakfast soup known as *pho*.

Government loudspeakers, mounted high overhead, now silent, would soon blare propaganda as well as instructions for daily exercise.

In an open area at the north end of Hoan Kiem Lake, an air defense crew, part of the Hanoi Air Defense Battalion, manned a dual-barrel 37mm gun.

Since the middle of June, American fighter-bombers flew over the distant periphery of Hanoi. Banshee screams of the planes' turbines and the frightening thunder of their exhaust, as well as bomb explosions, raged from the edge of the city.

The sharp explosive retorts of heavy air defense guns near the river, the rapid-fire machine-guns mounted on rooftops around the Yen Phu power plant, and the screech of missiles from earthen revetments near Phuc Yen airfield shook the outlying villages.

Men of the Hoan Kiem anti-aircraft unit were in action themselves. The area was littered with spent shell casings, the air redolent of lingering cordite fumes. The crew of eight men had been on duty all night, just like every night. In a moment of quiet stillness, the gunners, feeling confident they could do so, stepped away from their post to stretch, have something to eat and light a cigarette. They were never far from their gun.

On Hoa Lo Street, not yet benefitting from natural light, tree leaves didn't rustle. Fleeting grey ghost shadows soon appeared as a few people walked past guards standing outside Hoa Lo prison or stopped to visit near a concealed cooking fire. A young girl quietly pedaled her old bicycle, its bent wheels missing spokes, along the center of the street. She passed two old men with long pointed beards sitting on their haunches, each smoking a tobacco-stained dieu cay, an eighteen-inch bamboo pipe.

The onerous wood doors to the main prison entrance, located not quite in the middle of the short street, were solidly closed and well-guarded. Red and green glass shards from broken wine bottles protruded from the top of the high walls. Barbwire, strung along the sharp edges, adding to the peril, deterred escape attempts.

Inside the infamous prison, the so-called Hanoi Hilton, with its melancholy cells and interrogation rooms and algae-stained walls, forbidding darkness and unnerving silence prevailed.

The pervasive stench of human waste in the cell blocks was horrifically nauseating. Slop buckets reeked in cells without rudimentary toilet facilities. In the larger cells, the floors near the primitive cockroach-ridden toilets, just holes in the slab, were sticky wet. The sewers beneath the walkways overflowed with putrid black sludge.

Rats, the size of small dogs, coming out in dozens mostly at night, scurried throughout the prison and over the bodies of prisoners. The rats often bit the toes of captured American airmen. Mosquitos were prolific, their buzzing sound incessant.

Fighting with the vermin and the mosquitos, the airmen, some confined in leg irons that cut deep into their skin, sat in their damp concrete cells. Each American wore pajama-like prisoner uniforms stained with dirt and soaked in smelly, weeks-old sweat. The unshaven, frayed-looking men, many with diarrhea, were covered with scabs, tropical sores and festering boils that would subside only to return with hideous oozing yellow puss.

Some Americans suffered from horrific wounds—broken backs, compressed spinal discs and fractured arms and legs—as a result of ejecting from a stricken aircraft and a parachute landing in rough terrain. The brutal treatment and interrogations that followed only enhanced the pain and created new injuries.

While most Americans attempted to sleep, few really slept.

The American captives had nothing to look forward to during the day, or any day while in captivity ... except freedom. But release or escape was too remote to consider.

The sky over the Hoan Kiem gun crew, over Hoa Lo and all of Hanoi, soon transformed from the pervasive black of the endless heavens into a deep, dark azure-blue. It gave way to the sun rising silently in the eastern sky over the Gulf of Tonkin, spreading an amber light across the soft landscape of the Red River delta. The oppressive air was calm.

Hanoi sat gloomily beneath the low gossamer clouds amidst tranquil green rice fields. Shrouded in a faint glow, the tired city, holding no promise, no life, brightened briefly in the slanting, intermittent shafts of sunlight.

Each morning at 6:00 a.m., a Vietnamese guard in Hoa Lo's courtyard made a terrible racket which came to be known as the get-out-of-bed gong, though no gong was used at all. He banged on an expended artillery casing. This was the same bothersome signal for the go-to-bed gong that sounded each and every night after sunset.

On the morning of 6 July, the banging was more acute, more urgent. *Bong......Bong......Bong.*

The tempo increased.

Bong… bong… bong… bong.

Then.

Bongbongbongbong.

Paul Galanti had arrived at Hoa Lo blindfolded on the twenty-ninth of June. His hands were tied tightly behind his back. He had just experienced a rough eight-day journey in the back of a truck. Dehydrated and beat up, Galanti, lying on the concrete, was unable to move for days. He was just a soul occupying a battered body that had not stopped breathing.

On 6 July, Paul Galanti was still recovering from his ordeal when an obnoxious guard brusquely entered his cell and replaced a set of his blue prison garb with striped, khaki-colored clothes. Galanti noticed the alpha-numeric TU-31 on the shirt. Galanti knew some French. *Ah!* he thought. TU was short for *tuer*, the French verb meaning to kill. Galanti grimly concluded he had been handed his death sentence. These must be his execution clothes. While the numeral 31 could have represented he was thirty-first in line, Paul, in fact, didn't know what the number meant. Just a number, he supposed.

Alan Lurie and Darrel Pyle, who arrived at Hoa Lo on the same date as Galanti, heard the annoying wake-up gong. They were surprised later when their clothes were taken away and replaced with two sets of prison pajamas. Each shirt was numbered on the back. The American airmen, not knowing what to expect, were told to put on the strange clothes.

The Vietnamese gave Lurie sulfa powder for his infected feet and a cup of warm water and some sugar.

* * * *

Meanwhile, to the southwest of Hanoi, in an area not as densely populated as the central part of the city, guards at the Zoo began to stir. The heat and humidity made the air unpleasantly heavy. What sounded like trashcan or cooking pot lids were banged together. The sixth of July began in much the same fashion as at Hoa Lo.

On the other side of the prison wall, villagers were busy with morning chores. The noise caused by crowing roosters, clucking chickens and yapping dogs was endless. The disgusting sound of people coughing, snorting and relieving themselves along the roadway, created an unpleasant ambiance and assaulted the senses. A cacophony of high-pitched voices rose as merchants chatted with one another or shrieked across the street while they raised shutters to open their small shops.

Clanging noise from a mechanic's shed and the constant hammering from the tire repair shop provided abrupt ear-splitting sounds. The harshness of a power saw cutting through timber, the unending putt-putt of the *xe cong nong*, small one-cylinder diesel trucks, and the wafting smoke and odors from cooking fires contributed to the neighborhood's morning chaos.

Robbie Risner, transferred from Hoa Lo a few days before, now recovering from his time in leg irons, found the Zoo to be a step up. His new home was not as dreary as the old French prison. He was allowed to obtain fresh drinking water and to exercise for fifteen minutes each day.

The day before, on the fifth of July, Risner was forced to relinquish a set of clothes, the shirt of which had been stenciled with TU-31, the same alpha-numeric designation Paul Galanti had been issued at Hoa Lo. Risner received a replacement prisoner uniform with 570, a new number, on the back of the shirt.

Ray Merritt, a prisoner since September 1965, noticed changes in routine at the Zoo. On the fifth of July, guards took a set of Merritt's prison clothes. On the morning of the sixth, he received different clothes, the shirt of which had a number painted on the back. As far as Merritt knew, all the prisoners had been issued such shirts. He could attach no significance to the number. He asked what his fellow compatriots thought by tapping on the walls. Curiously, he learned not everyone had been given different shirts at all. He was also surprised to learn that some had received medicine for their ailments.

Cole Black, imprisoned first at Hoa Lo immediately after his shootdown on 21 June 1966, suffered through brutal interrogations before being transferred to the Zoo at the end of June. He didn't know the tap code, the environment or the mannerisms of the Zoo prison guards; or any of the Americans either.

During the day on the 6th of July, a guard opened Black's cell, spit on the floor and threw him long pants and a long-sleeve shirt. Pretty well incapacitated because of the interrogation beatings, Black stared blankly at the guard who then tossed a pair of charcoal-grey rubber-sole sandals made from old tires at his feet.

"What are these for?"

The guard left Black's cell without responding.

Alan Brunstrom was told to put on long pants and a long-sleeve prison shirt with a number. The Vietnamese guard, now standing in his cell, didn't know how to say long-sleeve shirt, but indicated the necessary clothing by making a slight open-palm chopping motion with one hand on the wrist of his other hand and the same motion at the ankles. Long sleeve shirt and long pants were the required attire.

Arthur Cormier had fallen asleep on the late evening of the fifth of July. The next thing he felt, before sunrise on the sixth, was a gun barrel prodding him. A guard was taking a set of his prison clothes. They were returned an hour later with three digits on the shirt.

On the morning of 6 July, guards unlocked Rob Doremus's cell door and entered. They tersely took a prisoner uniform. Later, a different uniform came back. *This is different*, Doremus thought. Whenever there was a change in routine, Doremus would speculate as to the implications and what it held for him and his comrades. *Now what?*

Larry Guarino, in the same cell with Ron Byrne, was beaten often but his inner strength, derived from his deep affection for his wife and family, his religious beliefs and his amusing personality, saw him through tough times. Guarino, finding ironic humor in every event, would utter to Byrne, "They don't scare me."

In one incident, an interrogator was continuously yelling at Guarino. Overly annoyed, Guarino stared at his antagonist.

"Do you realize you're talking to an officer in the United States Air Force?"

Guarino's assertive question, more a declaration of authoritative pride stated in a stentorian voice, caught the interrogator by surprise. Such impudence could not be tolerated by the prison officials. They beat Guarino until his face was bruised and swollen. His eyes closed shut.

One night in the middle of an American air strike beyond the outskirts of Hanoi, Guarino had an immediate need to squat over the slop bucket. The bomb explosions were loud and bright. They seemed to come from the next street. The screaming, thundering sound of the American jets shook the city. Guards were shocked when they saw a nonchalant, unbothered Guarino through the cell door.

On another occasion, a turnkey the Americans called Groucho, who had only a few teeth, entered Guarino's cell and flashed a toothless smile. Groucho talked about how the American air criminals must be brought to justice.

Larry Guarino smirked.

"Justice, my ass."

As the day broke on the sixth at the Zoo, the morning routines of Larry Guarino and his cellmate Ron Byrne were shattered. They were made to bathe at an abnormal time. Their tasks had to be urgently completed. The two men were issued new prisoner clothes. Guarino looked at the guard.

"What's with this number crap?"

Duffy Hutton could never figure out why he had become such a target of physical abuse especially since after many months, he still had nothing to offer. He was a Vigilante crew member off the USS *Independence* but the carrier had long since returned home. Nonetheless, he experienced the madness of the interrogators so often his body became numb. Often each week, keys would rattle, a fearful sound to all American prisoners, as his cell door was unlocked. Hutton knew what was about to transpire.

"Here we go again."

The questioning and beatings began anew.

Hutton was exposed to the cold for months. He had no blanket, no shoes. He slept on a cold concrete slab in his cell. While the North Vietnamese beat Duffy Hutton to his knees, it was the cold that made him the most miserable.

Like other prisoners at the Zoo, on 6 July 1966, Hutton was made to wear different prison garb.

Smitty Harris was told to shave after the so-called quiet hour. Sometime later, a shirt with a number was returned to him. A guard, his fingers mimicking a person in motion on the palm of his other hand, indicated he would be traveling.

Jerry Coffee, awakened by the gong at 6:00 a.m., was tersely instructed to shave by the guard who mimicked a shaving motion on his face. After being in prison for a year, Coffee knew a change, any change in routine equated to increased malice. He and his compatriots would no doubt suffer the results of some concocted rage.

Several guards came to Coffee's cell and ordered him to don the long-sleeve shirt.

"Put on. You silence. Not talk . . . and ready you."

Jerry Denton, who had spent the previous twelve months in solitary confinement, noticed that guards were tense, almost fearful, as they made their rounds.

The Zoo complex was abuzz with nervous tapping sounds on the walls. Urgently tapped messages among the Americans were persistent and loud. Woodpeckers couldn't have made more noise.

"We're changing camps."

A tap came back. "I think they're shuffling cell mates."

Yet another. "We're being moved around."

Another tapper's excitement was palpable given the speed with which he tapped his response.

"The war must be over."

The constant wall messaging raised hopes that the North Vietnamese had come to their senses. Spirits soared.

"We're going home!"

* * * *

Thirty-three miles northwest of Hanoi, near the Red River, another group of Americans imprisoned at Briar Patch started the day, too. They woke up to the sound of loud banging on a truck brake-drum that served as the camp gong.

Situated on a remote hillside, Briar Patch was bathed in sunrays slicing through the low clouds. The only excitement at Briar Patch was that of seeing smoke over the prison walls from village cooking fires dotting the countryside, hearing chirping birds and the noise of jet engines and responding anti-aircraft gunfire.

Everett Alvarez, a prisoner since August 1964 and now at Briar Patch, heard the explosions of bombs in late June 1966. He was not alone. Wes Schierman, Tom Barrett, Jim Bell, JB McKamey and others also heard the rumbling of distant bombing and were thrilled to know U.S. planes were overhead. American aviators were still on the job keeping pressure on the North Vietnamese.

Radio Hanoi was still on the job, too, denouncing the Yankee criminal air raids. Trinh Thi Ngo, better known as Hanoi Hannah, was in overdrive during her daily forty-five-minute broadcast when she talked into a microphone at the Hanoi radio station while smoking her *Tam Dao* cigarettes. Fluent in English, her deadpan voice emanated from loudspeakers mounted on bamboo poles in prison yards and in cell blocks, indeed throughout the streets of Hanoi. Annoying, her voice cut through the city and the prisons delivering scornful broadcasts about American airmen who, attacking her country, had dropped bombs on targets outside the Hanoi area.

As the Briar Patch guards dashed from cell to cell, they took prison clothes from some of the prisoners and instructed them to roll up their netting and sleeping mats. Later, toward noon, clothes were placed on the ground in a pile. The same prisoners were instructed to wear the uniforms lying at their feet.

Like the prisoners at Hoa Lo and the Zoo, each shirt was emblazoned with a number on the back. In the case of Everett Alvarez, his was 206.

If the number represented the quantity of American prisoners, Alvarez reasoned, then at least two hundred must have been captured. Alvarez thought, however, the quantity bogus since only a fourth of that many were incarcerated with him. Jim Bell's number was 312. Bill Tschudy's was 381.

Although all of the Americans at Hoa Lo, the Zoo and Briar Patch were experiencing commotion, suggesting some sort of change, they still faced another day of nothing. A few, however, would soon realize the sixth of July would be like no other.

The American prisoners waited. What else could they do?

CHAPTER 16

GREEN MILITARY TRUCKS

During the early-afternoon of 6 July 1966, two partially canvas-covered, green military trucks pulled inside the Briar Patch prison yard and squealed to a stop. The engines emitted blackish-brown smoke with the usual odor of incomplete combustion, the result of fouled injectors. Ed Davis heard voices, the scuffle of feet, truck doors open and close and tailgates clanging as they were let down.

A short time later, sixteen Briar Patch prisoners, out of a total of fifty-three, were assembled in the courtyard. Blindfolded and bound by the wrists in twos, the Americans were led to the two waiting trucks. Closely monitored by shouting, rifle-toting guards, the prisoners were forced to climb aboard the truck beds—difficult since the men couldn't see, awkward because one hand was tied to the hand of another person.

Jim Hivner and his mate Ed Davis were physically thrown into the back of a truck.

Two guards, their rifles at the ready, were positioned in each truck bed. Being much shorter than the Americans, who had to crouch as they climbed aboard, the guards' heads were just touching the underside of the trucks' canvas covers. Drawn taut, the heavy tarps completely enclosed the prisoners and guards. The temperature of the dark interiors soared.

The trucks, their worn-out engines belching diesel smoke, began to move slowly. They turned onto the highway toward Hanoi.

Tom Barrett, tied to Everett Alvarez in the truck, could see slightly from beneath his blindfold. However, he could only discern the silhouettes of fellow prisoners sitting next to him.

Barrett and Alvarez and the other bound men tapped or spoke softly while sneaking peeks of their surroundings.

At the outset of the trip, Wes Schierman made physical and verbal contact with others in the truck. Due to the darkness and the blindfold around his head, making out the face of each man was impossible, but Schierman immediately exchanged his name with his fellow prisoners.

Some Americans whispered among themselves.

"We're headed to the DMZ."

The captive airmen would be released; a glorious day. Others would follow.

But such wishful thoughts belied North Vietnam's strategic necessity of keeping all the Americans as future bargaining chips. Plus, a trip to the DMZ would take two weeks. Gia Lam, Hanoi's civil airport, would seem the more likely destination. If hostilities had ceased, the airmen would surely be released from there.

Being with Americans in the truck was a fleeting bright moment in what Jim Hivner, less optimistic, thought would probably be a bad ordeal. As the trucks bumped along the road to Hanoi, Hivner and Davis and other passengers, each still whispering, speculated a different fate. They thought they were headed for a Bertrand Russell war tribunal. Hanoi Hannah made such references in her listless voice.

Sucked through the canvas flaps into the back of the trucks, the road dust was stifling, the toxic exhaust, sickening.

The guards, desperate for air, opened the front flap of the tarp and pulled it to one side. They leaned over the cab into the wind. The in-rush of sunlight and fresher air proved a relief. The guards, facing forward, stood in the wind stream.

The Americans, breathing easier and taking note of the guards' lack of attention, talked freely. The conversations became lively. Feisty grab-ass ensued which brought muted laughter and smiles to the prisoners' faces.

A guard turned and, seeing the Americans exploiting their good fortune, began to kick them. He singled out Ron Storz, the tallest American, and gave him plenty of kicks to his thighs and slaps to his face. He yelled at Storz.

"You air pirate, not talk!"

JB McKamey couldn't see of course but he was sure he'd be the next target. The guards kicked his shins a few times then left him alone.

In a moment of comic relief, Jerry Singleton, seated on a bench in the truck bed, laughed when he heard someone say out loud to a guard: "Your mother wears combat boots and chases the base bus."

Singleton never learned who made the comment but he heard the reprisal on the guilty party.

The Vietnamese guards in the truck yelled at the prisoners.

"Not good attitude! Will die!"

The airmen, continuing to communicate, received again quick hard slaps to their faces and kicks to their thighs. A guard tapped several Americans on their heads with the butt of his rifle.

"Silence!"

The Americans would be quiet for a moment then start again, whispering at first, but becoming louder and louder until they received the slapping, kicking, no-talk routine from the guards.

The blindfolded, partially trussed-up men, unable to defend themselves, could not anticipate when or from where the next blow would come. But wanting to communicate, the abuse wasn't a deterrent to keep them from talking during the ride.

Near Hanoi, an air raid siren screamed. The drivers searched anxiously for a place to hide the trucks. They pulled off the road and stopped in a covered area.

Ed Davis, setting up a diversion to warn his companions to be quiet, yelled to one of the guards that he had to empty his bladder badly.

"I gotta go!"

The guard retorted angrily.

"Why you talk?"

Davis, having a bit of fun, continued.

"Because I gotta pee right now damnit!"

The guard's fist slammed into the side of Davis's head. Davis couldn't help but grin.

"You know, I don't have to go so bad now."

Jim Hivner, Tom Barrett, Everett Alvarez and other American truck occupants laughed at Davis's antics.

Within an hour, the trucks started to roll again.

After what seemed an everlasting time, the two trucks from Briar Patch entered Hanoi and made their way to a sports stadium where the prisoners were off-loaded.

Ed Davis, never losing his sense of humor, looked from beneath his blindfold.

"Well, the Christians are here. Where are the lions?"

Hivner, Davis's mate, equally unable to see, responded humorously, "Oh yeah, they're here."

Taken inside a structure, each blindfolded American was fed an old banana and a handful of rice along with a cup of water.

The earlier unfounded optimism of freedom quickly faded to despair. The Briar Patch prisoners who hoped to be freed, realized they were not going to be released. They knew something else was in store for them.

The bound Americans from Briar Patch loaded again on board the two trucks and departed the stadium in the early evening.

* * * *

The situation at the Zoo, located closer in but on the outskirts of Hanoi, was similar to what transpired at Briar Patch a few hours before. The day passed tediously.

The selected prisoners who received new shirts were under tight security. At mid-afternoon, they were fed boiled greens, stale rice balls and raw morsels of meat.

Robbie Risner saw prisoners being taken one-by-one to an office across the courtyard. The guards eventually came for him. They instructed Risner to put on the long-sleeve uniform with the new number. Risner was blindfolded then led to the office.

Jerry Denton, wearing the set of pajama prison clothes he had been given, was removed from his cell. Blindfolded, Denton was taken to the office and handcuffed to another prisoner. He learned through the tap code that his mate was Bob Peel.

Having been told to wear the new clothes, Zoo prisoners Smitty Harris, Bob Shumaker, Bruce Seeber and Rob Doremus were eventually taken from their cells and led to the same office where others were being assembled.

Later that day, trucks passed through the Zoo prison gates, bounded by large brick columns on either side, and rumbled into the compound. Ray Merritt, Arthur Cormier, Jerry Coffee and Alan Brunstrom heard the vehicles roll past the dilapidated shed where prisoners toil with mindless tasks. The trucks stopped not far from Cole Black's cell. Black could not discern how many vehicles had arrived but by the noise, he thought maybe three. The motors were turned off. The courtyard fell silent, only to be filled with Vietnamese voices.

Three hours before sundown, armed guards came to Porter Halyburton's cell and brusquely told him he must "dress serious." Halyburton needed to put on the long sleeve shirt thrown at him that morning. Then, he was taken to join the others.

Later, the bound Americans were led from the assembly building to the courtyard near the pool and forced to load into the trucks. There they waited.

Porter Halyburton could see somewhat from under his blindfold. He quickly learned he and his mate Arthur Burer were not alone as they sat in the truck.

A guard entered Cole Black's cell and motioned for Black to replace the clothes he was wearing with the long pants, long-sleeve shirt and sandals he had been given earlier. The unwashed uniform was old and smelly.

The guard left for a short period of time and returned with two other guards. They opened the door to Black's cell. One of the guards spoke.

"You have work to do."

Cole Black smiled as an expression of slight excitement swept over his face. Since his shootdown on 21 June, two weeks before, work or no work, whatever the Vietnamese wanted him to do would result in some sort of distraction, perhaps his first "liberty."

There was, however, a stern warning. A guard poked Black in his side with a gun barrel.

"You talk, you shot."

Taken from his restricting cubicle, Black, blindfolded, was led directly to the courtyard. He heard loud Vietnamese voices. He was tied to a prisoner at the wrist and made to climb up a short steep ramp into the back of a truck.

Jerry Driscoll and Chuck Boyd were handcuffed together, blindfolded and loaded directly into a second truck. They were forced to sit on the truck bed near the tailgate.

Ron Byrne and Larry Guarino were taken from their cell late in the afternoon. Once outside, the Vietnamese secured their sandals to their feet with gauze. They were taken straight to the waiting trucks to join their comrades.

Boyd exchanged whispered words with his fellow Americans. A guard rapped his head hard.

The American airmen, communicating with the tap code, were enclosed by a heavy tarp. The heat inside, quickly rising to well above one hundred degrees, was broiling.

In addition to the prisoners, three guards were in each truck. The Americans called one of them Dum Dum because he looked like a dullard and acted dumb. Just as the truck motor started,

Dum Dum waved his pistol at everyone's blindfolded face and tapped their heads with the muzzle.

"You talk truck, you shot like creemeenal."

At such close range, the bullet wouldn't miss.

The guards told the American prisoners they were going someplace new.

Rob Doremus whispered, "Like where? Disneyland?"

Some Zoo prisoners, similar to their comrades earlier at Briar Patch, now openly concluded they were going to be released.

Larry Guarino, in the back of a truck along with the others, blindfolded with his hands bound, listened to some of his comrades who expressed hope for release. Others voiced anxiety.

Guarino reacted sanguinely: "They ain't gonna do shit."

The Russian-made trucks with thirty Americans on board rolled outside the Zoo prison gate bound for the so-called new place.

* * * *

Back in town at Hoa Lo, four prisoners—Alan Lurie, Darrel Pyle, Paul Galanti and Leonard Eastman—each wearing a numbered shirt, departed the city prison before sundown. Their destination was not revealed.

THE HANOI MARCH

CHAPTER 17

GET OUT! – NHA HAT LON HA NOI

Trucks carrying the Briar Patch prisoners, followed a circuitous route from the stadium to Pho Le Thanh Tong while the Zoo trucks, making a slightly longer drive, rumbled through the streets of Hanoi to the same destination. From not even a mile away, the Hoa Lo prisoners, driven to the same place, joined those from the other two facilities.

Each truck bounced over a curb into an open park-like area and came to a stop. Unbeknownst to the bound Americans, they had arrived at a downtown plaza next to Nha Hat Lon Ha Noi, the fifty-year-old Hanoi Opera House.

The open area was awash in fumes, the smell of engine oil and diesel fuel. The unmuffled drone of a nearby generator added its own noise to the confusion.

Faint floodlights provided a weak but ominous light. Shadows, following each person as he moved, crowded the setting with phantom surrogates.

Vietnamese army officers, barking at the drivers, walked hurriedly around each truck. Guards unlocked and dropped the tailgates which made a loud bang as they hit the trucks' undercarriage. The flaps of the tarps of each truck were pulled back to reveal masses of sweating, emaciated Americans, like sardines in a can, wearing prison pajamas and sandals made from old tires.

The guards yelled, "Get out!"

Sixteen Americans from Briar Patch began to stand up to a crouch. Urged by the guards to descend from the back of the trucks, they cursed out loud.

"How the hell can we climb down blindfolded and our hands tied? We'll break our friggin' necks."

The Americans from the Zoo and Hoa Lo, still blindfolded, also struggled to climb down from each truck bed to the ground. Unable to support themselves with their hands tied and no visibility, some almost fell.

To ease such a calamity for Cole Black, a guard abruptly yanked his blindfold to his chin causing his head to snap forward. His eyes adjusted to the glare of the lights in the surrounding dimness. Black was careful not to trip as he climbed down from the truck. He quickly saw many Americans in the immediate area. Chaos and simultaneous loud voices were all around him. Black didn't have time to make sense of the muddle. He was re-blindfolded.

Now, out of the truck, Ron Storz, from Briar Patch, was vocal.

"OK guys, let's stand tall."

Vietnamese officials who milled around the prisoners were under the control of Nguyen Minh Y, better known as the Rabbit.

Rabbit yelled orders as he looked at the blindfolded, expressionless men.

"Not talk! You quiet!"

Wearing his uniform and pith helmet, an adopted remnant of colonial days when French officials displayed their white *casque coloniale*, Rabbit walked among the blindfolded Americans now huddled together. He issued instructions to the guards to untether certain pairs. Their wrists were freed but were then re-tied or handcuffed to a new partner. Rabbit, checking a list, began to arrange the men side-by-side in a predetermined order.

A guard standing near Jon Reynolds asked him if he needed to make water, but Reynolds didn't understand the question. Bob Purcell, standing to Reynold's right, abruptly piped up, "He wants to know if you wanna piss!"

Jerry Coffee and Art Cormier, neither one knowing beforehand they would be tied together, were isolated several feet from the main body of prisoners. Coffee, peering through the bottom of his blindfold, tried to find Bob Hansen, the naval flight officer of his Vigilante. Coffee thought he had been captured in the water off the coast after he ejected. Coffee's vision, however, was too limited by the blindfold. He didn't see Hansen.

Chuck Boyd and Jerry Driscoll, still blindfolded, were uncuffed and told to make water. Then, Boyd was recuffed to Jerry Driscoll, or so Boyd assumed. The pair was guided by a guard on each side and positioned in a formation with others.

The Rabbit talked through his bullhorn which he perhaps used as compensation for his short height when standing next to the giant Americans.

"You shilent stay."

Satisfied all was in order, Rabbit, letting his guard down, having forgotten to compensate for his dialect, issued another instruction to the blindfolded prisoners.

"Shit down."

Each American with a partner at his side and guards close by, bent over, felt for the pavement and sat down on the hot, grimy asphalt of Pho Le Thanh Tong.

Larry Guarino, not knowing what to expect, turned to his mate Ron Byrne. "Well," Guarino said with obvious sarcasm, "here we are shittin' in some street in Hanoi."

Byrne smiled and shook his head: *Thank God for Larry Guarino.*

Al Brudno turned right to Bill Tschudy.

"What's next?"

"Damned if I know," Tschudy responded. "What a circus."

Still blindfolded, Everett Alvarez thought he was still tied to Tom Barrett, but he wasn't completely sure. He mumbled to his partner, "Who are you?"

The man next to him whispered, "Robbie Risner."

Surprised and impressed he was now partnered with such a famous aviator, Alvarez told him who he was.

Risner wanted to know from which camp Alvarez came.

"Briar Patch."

Risner inquired as to how he was holding up. Alvarez indicated he was fine, his spirits high.

After some time, the hand-bound prisoners were instructed to stand up from their sitting position. They were oriented in the same direction—straight forward. One by one, the blindfolds were removed from each American's face.

Bill Tschudy looked nervously to each side. Out of the corner of his eye, he saw his comrades standing in a line behind him. He quickly turned to face forward and, because no prisoners stood in front of him, realized he and Al Brudno, standing to his left, were leading a column of his countrymen.

"We're at the head of a line. What the hell are the V doing?"

Farther back, the captives tried to gain a sense of locale but due to dense crowds, they couldn't see far. They communicated discreetly with the other prisoners, some of whom they had never before seen or heard. This incurred the anger of the Vietnamese guards who immediately began slapping the backs of their heads and shouting at them.

"You not look side. You shot."

Pistols, often pointed at the Americans, were waved carelessly. Dum Dum never holstered his.

While the Rabbit was busy organizing the lineup, North Vietnamese army officers and Cong An (security officials) scurried about shouting orders at guards and lower-ranking officers thereby adding to the disorderly scene.

Trucks, filling the air with foul exhaust and the irritating, distinctive sound of diesel engines, entered and left the area.

Many of the captives wore a cloth strap around their feet so as not to lose their rubber flip-flop sandals.

Never failing to exhort ominous instructions while showing off, Rabbit fearlessly and arrogantly walked among the paired prisoners. He enjoyed the status of being able to control Americans who were much bigger than him.

The Rabbit raised the bullhorn to his mouth and yelled into it.

"You shee hatred now people Vietnam."

Bob Purcell turned left to Jon Reynolds.

"Oh goodie. Can't wait."

A Vietnamese guard nicknamed Mickey Mouse, careful not to upstage the Rabbit, told Alan Brumstrom and Render Crayton and other American prisoners that the Vietnamese people were intending to show them their anger. Further, the criminals would be executed if they talked.

To Jerry Singleton, having arrived at the assembly point from Briar Patch, the gathering was a typical military event: hurry up and wait.

Jim Hivner and his mate Ed Davis spoke in soft whispers but were caught, slapped and warned not to talk again.

Davis, remembering the humor during the trip from Briar Patch earlier that day, muttered sarcastically, "Good God."

Jerry Coffee, tied to Art Cormier, standing to his right, caught sight of trees, bushes and flowers adjacent to where they were standing. Coffee was reminded of family picnics in a Modesto city park. His grandmother would lay out potluck meals—dishes of fried chicken, baked beans, potato salad and ice tea—on a large checkered cloth she spread on the ground while kids played on the grass.

Art Cormier, the only enlisted man in the group, turned his head to the left but was warned by a guard.

"You straight look."

Cormier, trying to comprehend the situation, spoke to Coffee: "Holy shit, man! This is not going to be good!"

Coffee whispered back to Cormier, "Whatever happens, let's take good care of each other. Hang on tight. It's the only way we can survive whatever this thing is."

A Scandinavian man with long hair yelled at Coffee, "Yankee criminal son-of-a-bitch." The man hurled more vile remarks before working his way along the unmoving column.

Fifteen thousand Vietnamese people were watching the unfolding drama. Factory workers and construction laborers dressed alike in blue dungarees stood in groups.

The Rabbit spoke again to the unkempt Americans.

"You come know determine people Vietnam. We win war. You learn, but not maybe."

Rabbit's comment—"but not maybe"—caught the attention of Wendy Rivers.

Rivers took this to mean either collaborate and be rewarded or resist and be executed, ironically the same choice offered to the Americans weeks later.

Wes Schierman remained calm. His funny, yet sometimes dry sense of humor was as much a part of him as was his genuine, friendly smile. He laughed at the Rabbit.

Ron Storz, standing to Schierman's left, asked Schierman why he was laughing. Schierman, smiling coolly, responded, "Does Rabbit really think I give a rat's ass about what he says?"

The American prisoners were assembled in a line in two groups with a large gap in between.

Chuck Boyd and his mate, for some reason still wearing blindfolds, were the last pair in the first group while Howie Dunn and Ray Merritt led the second group.

To Alan Brumstrom, it appeared he and Render Crayton were the second pair in what he also thought was a second group of Americans. He could not see behind to know for sure the names or number of the men who followed.

The Scandinavian man who had yelled at Jerry Coffee now stood in front of Tom Barrett. Amidst the loud turmoil, he screamed at the line of Americans.

"You don't deserve to live, you bastards. You're all shit."

While the prisoners were held stationary, the scurrying movements and voices of Vietnamese officials, civilians and guards smoking and brandishing rifles with fixed bayonets, caused a continuous, loud commotion in the assembly area next to the Hanoi Opera House.

Military officers walked hurriedly around gesticulating and yelling at subordinates.

A number of photographers mixed in with the crowd. One man trained his camera on Robbie Risner and Everett Alvarez standing together, third in line, with glum yet defiant expressions on their faces. Their blindfolds had just been yanked from their heads. Alvarez looked warily at someone in front while Risner looked at the camera. Kile Berg and Pop Keirn stood eight feet behind them. The photographer snapped the picture.

Robbie Risner mumbled cynically to Alvarez, "This is all for show."

Duffy Hutton, in the middle of the lineup with Wendy Rivers, explained to a guard that he had to relieve himself. The guard left. A moment later he returned and pointed to the ground.

"Make here."

Hutton, turning to Rivers, laughed.

"I mean, he had to go check? Couldn't he just tell me that?"

Hutton, with slight embarrassment, proceeded to relieve himself in the middle of the crowd. Rivers couldn't contain his laughter.

A one-story house sat across the street on the opposite side of an open area in which there were a few trees. Across the front of the house stretched a wide veranda. JB McKamey, left of Paul Kari, in front of Hutton and Rivers, thought of farmsteads back home in Indiana. Two men, casual in their movements, as if relaxing, loitered on the veranda smoking cigarettes. They seemed oblivious to the hubbub ensuing not far away. The scene, amidst a larger foreboding ambiance that enveloped the area, was so inviting, McKamey fantasized he could join them perhaps with a cigar and a cognac. But, his station in life at that moment, vastly different from what he was observing, immediately precluded such baseless make-believe.

Rabbit, using his bullhorn, continued to lecture the linear congregation of handcuffed American prisoners.

"You experience hatred Vietnam people. Must apologize."

The bullhorn magnified his shrill, angry voice and exacerbated his strident, awkward English.

"Orders obey. Courtesy show, or danger. Remember. Creemeenal, you!"

The Rabbit paused, then said with more vehemence, "Tonight, we take you inquiry public."

Another pause, then, "You shee indignation people Vietnam."

Duffy Hutton turned his head to Wendy Rivers.

"Indignation?" Duffy said, inflecting his voice. "Rabbit must have practiced that word a lot."

"And what's more, he gets to use it," Wendy responded while chuckling.

Rabbit continued his stern harangue, warning the American prisoners with ominous instructions.

"If people want harm you, we not shtop people."

Larry Guarino was fed up.

"Can we just get on with it?"

The Rabbit's verbal rants became so repetitive, the Americans, unmoved, paid scant attention. However, his one statement about public inquiries sent shivers through many of the airmen. The rumor must be true. They were going to be publicly tried in a kangaroo court and summarily shot by firing squad. The crowd would watch as the Americans paid with their lives.

Two days before, an announcement circulated around Hanoi from loudspeakers in the districts and neighborhoods of the city. The citizens of Hanoi were going to be treated to a grand spectacle. In the evening, starting at the opera house, the Americans were to be exhibited.

It seemed all of North Vietnam was now congregated in one

area. People stood everywhere, along the sidewalks, on store stoops and on balconies. The intersections were jammed with jubilant but mad North Vietnamese.

The Hanoi Opera House faced a straight street that disappeared in the vague distance. The long avenue, previously called Rue Paul Bert during French colonial days, now Pho Trang Tien, was lined with fully-packed bleachers.

The Americans, handcuffed or tied in pairs, now assembled and standing quietly in a stationary column next to the opera house, were surrounded by a discord of excited, angry voices. They waited for the next move.

Stone-faced guards, carrying rifles with bayonets, stood to either side of each pair and warily eyed the Americans. Inexperienced and nervous, the young soldiers wore new uniforms and pith helmets with the insignia of North Vietnam on the front above the brim.

Shafts of sharp light from flashlights darted through the crowds.

The Rabbit, now standing in front of Al Brudno and Bill Tschudy at the lead, pleased to be the center of attention, scrunched up his nose with obvious smugness. He raised his voice for all to hear.

"Creemeenal aggressor pirates. World know you crime."

The line of Americans stood still.

Rabbit depressed the button on his bullhorn again.

"Do not harm people. Do not talk people. You touch people, you killed. Bow head and respect show."

Then, in the darkness, well after sundown on Wednesday, the sixth of July 1966 in North Vietnam's capital city, the Rabbit, with the bullhorn still to his mouth, depressed the talk button again triggering what would come to be known as the Hanoi March.

"Now, you walk."

THE HANOI MARCH

PART THREE

PARADES AND OTHER DISPLAYS

THE HANOI MARCH

CHAPTER 18

HISTORICAL CONTEXT

North American natives were not known to have parades. Instead, they had ceremonies usually around campfires observed by the entire tribe. While wearing headdress and regalia unique to their tribe, with faces painted in various colors, they performed ancient, sacred dances to the beat of drums. At least, these are the images seen in Western films.

Hollywood dramatized the war dance in movies to connote impending battle. However, the war dance was only one of many dances, not the most important one. American Indians celebrated many events through dance. Harvests, good hunting, marriage, fertility, birth and death were a few. Indian dances were sometimes a tribute to earth, wind and fire and an invocation for rain.

In the late 1600s and early 1700s, Europeans brought the concept of the parade to what came to be called the United States. During more contemporary times, the Rose Bowl Parade, Mardi Gras parades and Macy's Thanksgiving Day Parade, each fanciful and joyous, became traditions.

Every four years, the United States experiences the president's inaugural parade in Washington, D.C. where representatives of each branch of service and every state pass by the president's reviewing stand to much applause.

Military parades, often referred to as marches, are different for different reasons. Not inviting the direct involvement of or communion with gleeful bystanders, a military parade, dramatic in its execution, is something to behold.

During face-to-face conflicts, discipline within rank and file, organized by crisp audible orders, often proved the advantage. Lines of men in companies, battalions and regiments— the order of battle—had to be maintained if an army was to overcome its opponent. The skill of marching thousands of men in columns to a field of battle and then arranging them in lines to face the enemy was neither casual nor spontaneous.

Today's military parading, an outgrowth of those warring maneuvers, is a carefully executed artform. The precision of ritualistic drill, with ceremonial swords and other weaponry, exaggerated footwork and sharp, arcane verbal instructions, are captivating.

The awe-inspiring Evening Parade and attendant Silent Drill on the Quadrangle under floodlights at Marine Corps Barracks in Washington D.C. are spectacular and dazzling, a testament to the heritage of the United States Marine Corps.

"Voila Le Boudin" (Blood Sausage) is proudly sung by the French Foreign Legion during their parades. Legionnaires are conspicuous by the white hat known as *kepi* and green ties and epaulettes. Their somber parades are conducted at an incredibly exact cadence of eighty-eight steps per minute.

The somber Soviet Union May Day parade in Moscow each year reminded the world that the strength of the military force on display can be used at any time.

China showcased its military through an impressive parade in Beijing to mark the seventy-fifth anniversary of its revolution. Thousands of soldiers, sailors and special forces-type individuals marched in large blocks in precise lockstep and in perfect alignment while jets flew overhead. The fast-paced show was jaw-dropping.

The grandest, perhaps most splendid military display, celebrating the fall of the Bastille prison, is held every year on 14 July in Paris, France. Colorful uniforms and the exacting commands of

French officers, whose salutes outclass all others, resulting in disciplined regimental responses, are stirring, making the day-long event the length of l'Avenue des Champs-Élysées remarkable.

Akin to the grand shows of military parades, a reverse phenomenon with the same motive exists: Not the victorious, but rather the defeated are put on public display. There can be no more of a humiliation for a failed force than to be exhibited in submissive formation by the victors.

History is replete with such accounts.

Colossians 2:15 states: *Having disarmed principalities and powers, he made a public spectacle of them, triumphing over them in it.*

A variation, but taken to extremes, during 600-700 BC in China, the soldiers of Duke Mu of Qin severed heads of their enemies and put them on gruesome shows in public places—a static, dreadful parade of the vanquished.

In the first century BC, Celtic fighters claimed the heads of the fiercest opponents of their defeated enemies after battle and paraded them atop long sticks.

Armed forces of Montenegro, near the Dinaric Mountains, used the unfinished tower of Tablja, started in 1830, to exhibit hundreds of Turkish heads taken in battle.

In 1931 in Taiwan, one hundred severed heads of the Seediq were hideously arrayed in a square for ceremonial purposes after the Second Musha Incident.

Perhaps the most dreadful spectacle occurred two thousand years ago. A revolt of slaves took place against the Roman Empire. Led by a gladiator named Spartacus who used unorthodox combat tactics, an army of thousands of scurrilous rebels amassed to take on a fight they were destined to lose.

The Roman Senate gave mandate to Marcus Licinius Crassus, a new commander, to terminate Spartacus's rebellion and end the threat to Rome. Crassus commanded eight legions totaling fifty thousand Roman soldiers.

The final battle in 71 BC ensued near the town of Quaglietta in

Senerchia. Spartacus was killed soon after the fighting began, his army eventually defeated.

As a public display of victory, six thousand survivors captured by Crassus were executed on makeshift crosses lining the Appian Way, the road from Rome to Capua. The victors, gazing up at the distorted dead faces, paraded past the crucified enemy. The dominance of Rome was absolute.

One hundred thirty years later, in 31AD, Jesus Christ was marched through the streets of Jerusalem prior to his death. He was publicly executed on the cross he was forced to carry.

Beginning on 9 April 1942, immediately after the fall of Bataan in the Philippines, the Japanese marched sixty-five thousand Filipino and American soldiers from Marivale on the Bataan Peninsula to a rail head at San Fernando. The forced march covered eighty-six miles in six days. Seven hundred Americans and five thousand Filipinos died enroute.

Bivouacked in Montebon, France, the German 2nd SS Panzer Division, named *Das Reich*, was ordered to move north to Normandy to counter the Allied landing on 6 June 1944. The division's movements were hampered by the harassment of French Maquisards.

On 9 June, in retribution for the killing of forty German soldiers by the French Resistance, *Das Reich* hung ninety-nine Frenchmen from street lights and balconies along the main thoroughfare of Tulle situated on the Correze River in the Limouzin region of France. Villagers were made to look up as they were forced to march past the hanging bodies.

Beginning two weeks later on 23 June 1944 on the Eastern Front, the Soviet Union initiated an offensive codenamed Operation Bagration, the opening phase of the invasion of eastern Germany. The Russians completely destroyed Germany's Army Group Center in Belarus which, along with accompanying SS divisions, lost more than five hundred thousand soldiers.

Even though Operation Bagration was not finished, Stalin, flush with impending success, marched the survivors of the defeated

German army—sixty thousand of them!—through the streets of Moscow on 17 July 1944.

The "Great Waltz," the name the Russians gave the Moscow ex-hibit, borrowed from an American movie popular in the Soviet Union, was intended to bolster the demoralized spirit of the Soviet citizenry.

Huge crowds gathered to watch the procession of the captured German army that was arrayed in large blocks each of thirty rows with twenty soldiers per row, a total of six hundred men per block. One hundred blocks of German humanity marched past Soviet on-lookers along the wide boulevards of Moscow.

Prior to the massive display, the German prisoners were not al-lowed to wash. They were to appear as scrounging, flea-infested dogs. The Germans were fed boiled cabbage, intended to act as a fast-acting laxative, an added humiliation.

After the parade, the route was immediately washed down with water trucks. The cabbage soup worked as planned.

The men of German Army Group Center, never allowed to see Germany again, would perish in concentration camps far to the east of the Ural Mountains.

Immediately after the "Great Waltz" in Moscow, German high mil-itary officials, not to be outdone, hastily organized their own march of prisoners. Herded through Paris, captured U.S. and British sol-diers were put on public display even as the German occupiers were packing to leave. Much smaller in scope than the Moscow parade and hastily organized, the show was a feeble attempt to highlight German power, when in fact it was fast declining.

THE HANOI MARCH

PART FOUR

THE HANOI MARCH

THE HANOI MARCH

ORDER OF MARCH

Hanoi, Vietnam • 6 July 1966

The pairings and Order of March are believed to be an accurate representation based on available documents, recollections, books, personal interviews and accounts. AF=Air Force, MC=Marine Corps, N=Navy.

Position	Left	Right

First Group

	Left	Right
1.	Al Brudno (AF/BPatch)	Bill Tschudy (N/BPatch)
2.	Phil Butler (N/BPatch)	Hayden Lockhart (AF/BPatch)
3.	Robbie Risner (AF/Zoo)*	Ev Alvarez (N/BPatch)
4.	Kile Berg (AF/Zoo)	Pop Keirn (AF/Zoo)
5.	Smitty Harris (AF/Zoo)	Bob Shumaker (N/Zoo)
6.	Larry Guarino (AF/Zoo)	Ron Byrne (AF/Zoo)
7.	Bill Shankel (N/Zoo)	Richard Ratzlaff (N/Zoo)
8.	Jon Reynolds (AF/Zoo)	Bob "Percy" Purcell (AF/Zoo)
9.	JB McKamey (N/BPatch)	Paul Kari (AF/BPatch)
10.	Wendy Rivers (N/Zoo)	Duffy Hutton (N/Zoo)
11.	David Hatcher (AF/Zoo)	Larry Spencer (N/Zoo)
12.	Jerry Denton (N/Zoo)	Bob Peel (AF/Zoo)
13.	Cole Black (N/Zoo)	Chuck Boyd (AF/Zoo)

Second Group

	Left	Right
14.	Howie Dunn (MC/Zoo)	Ray Merritt (AF/Zoo)
15.	Alan Brunstrom (AF/Zoo)	Render Crayton (N/Zoo)
16.	Art Burer (AF/Zoo)	Porter Halyburton (N/Zoo)
17.	Tom Barrett (AF/BPatch)	Jerry Driscoll (AF/Zoo)
18.	Jerry Coffee (N/Zoo)	Art Cormier (AF/Zoo)
19.	Bruce Seeber (N/Zoo)	Rob Doremus (N/Zoo)
20.	Leonard Eastman (N/Hoa Lo)	Paul Galanti (N/Hoa Lo)
21.	Skip Brunhaver (N/BPatch)	Jerry Singleton (AF/BPatch)
22.	Edward Davis (N/BPatch)	Jim Hivner (AF/BPatch)
23.	Ron Storz (AF/BPatch)	Wes Schierman (AF/BPatch)
24.	Alan Lurie (AF/Hoa Lo)	Darrel Pyle (AF/Hoa Lo)
25.	Jim Bell (N/BPatch)	Ralph Gaither (N/BPatch)

*Robbie Risner was transferred from Hoa Lo to the Zoo just days before the march.

ROUTE OF HANOI MARCH

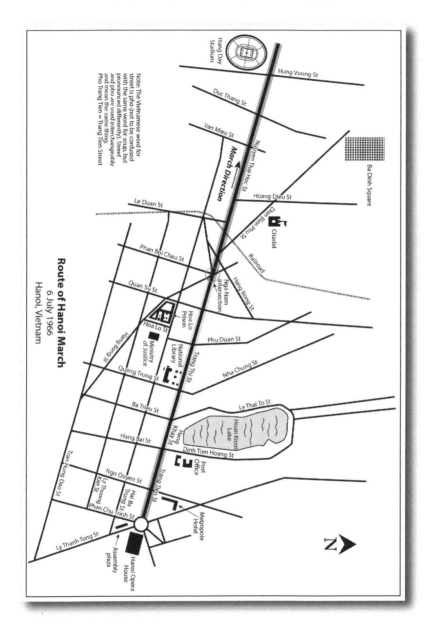

Map of route of the march through Hanoi. Direction of march is from right to left, beginning at the Hanoi Opera House. (*Drawing not to scale.*)

CHAPTER 19

FROM LIGHT – PHO TRANG TIEN

The Rabbit turned to face in the same direction as Al Brudno and Bill Tschudy and forty-eight Americans behind them. He climbed into a motorcycle sidecar and sat facing backward with the bullhorn in his hands. So pleased with his accomplishments, almost giddy, Rabbit was smiling from ear to ear.

Bill Tschudy turned slightly to his left and mumbled to Al Brudno.

"I'm sure they're going to try to make us bow our heads."

Tschudy was correct.

As the motorcycle moved forward slowly, Rabbit spoke into the bullhorn's mouthpiece in English.

"Bow head! Eyes forward! Keep shilence!"

Guards on each side prodded the two lead Americans. Brudno and Tschudy, their heads upright, put one foot in front of the other and slowly proceeded north in front of the Hanoi Opera House.

Twenty-five tethered pairs of Americans, like the legs of a centipede, began to shuffle along the pavement.

Wisecracks among the prisoners erupted in subdued voices.

Bob Purcell, to the right of Jon Reynolds, in eighth position, couldn't help himself.

"Oh, I love a parade."

The Americans near Purcell had difficulty maintaining a straight face.

Brudno and Tschudy followed the slow-moving motorcycle counterclockwise around a traffic circle past the elegant entrance to the opera house. Spectators, sitting on temporary bleachers on each side of the street, rose to their feet and, with loud voices, began shaking their fists at the American captives.

Robbie Risner, in third position, turned to his right and spoke to Everett Alvarez.

"Don't make any gestures. Just walk straight."

Alvarez nodded his understanding and added, "That's Butler and Lockhart in front of us."

Alvarez repeated it again. A guard caught him.

"Not talk!"

Alvarez turned his head to see who was behind, but another guard saw him.

"You straight look!"

Jerry Denton, tied on his right to Bob Peel, in twelfth position, passed the word around.

"Bounce back. Whatever happens, bounce back."

Denton saw a movie camera pointed at him. He made the "V" for victory sign.

The blindfolds of Chuck Boyd and his mate, marching behind Denton, had not been removed. A guard abruptly ripped them off.

Three quarters around the traffic circle, Brudno and Tschudy were led to the right through a slit in the bleachers opening the way west to Pho Trang Tien, Hanoi's most famous avenue. The line of pajama-clad Americans followed.

Rabbit's bullhorn continued to blast from the front.

"Bow head now!"

Jerry Denton shouted loudly, "We are Americans! Keep your heads up! Do not bow!"

Then, there was a duel between Denton, the tall American

dressed in drab prison clothes, and Rabbit, the much shorter, much younger Vietnamese, wearing a rumpled military uniform.

"You bow!"

"Keep your heads up!"

"Bow head!"

"Keep your heads up! Do not bow!"

Denton thrust his hand into the air and, extending his middle finger, casually flipped the bird.

Paul Kari, to the right of JB McKamey, three positions in front of Denton, scoffed at the Vietnamese instructions. His emphatic retort was clear: "I am not bowing my head. I've never been prouder to be an American than I am right now."

Farther back, a guard smacked Chuck Boyd on the back of his head, then yelled at him.

"Bow!"

Boyd was sure that was the only English word the soldier knew. He also knew he was not going to lower his head.

"Bullshit," the American uttered.

Boyd held his head as high as possible. From his peripheral vision to the left, Boyd thought he saw Jerry Driscoll next to him with his head lower than his. Since Driscoll was his same height, Boyd thought Driscoll was bowing. Boyd scorned, "Hold your head up, damnit. Don't bow!"

Another guard hit both men on the top of their heads with the flat side of a bayonet.

"No talk! Head put down!"

Chuck Boyd, turning slightly left, caught fleeting sight of what he thought was Driscoll's head still lowered.

"Hold your Goddamn head up!"

But something wasn't right. Boyd took another look and, surprised, saw he wasn't tethered to Jerry Driscoll at all, but rather to a shorter man who was holding his head as proudly high as he was. Chuck Boyd was embarrassed by his mistake.

"Oh, shit," Boyd said. "Sorry."

Chuck Boyd had just met Cole Black, shot down only days before. Each came to regard the other as the most important person in the world. The two men would depend on each other during the rest of the night. Black and Boyd, who didn't learn each other's name until sometime later, became brothers at that moment.

Jerry Driscoll, Boyd's original mate during the truck ride from the Zoo, was tied to the right of Tom Barrett, himself originally tied to Everett Alvarez during the trip from Briar Patch. Driscoll and Barrett were four places behind Black and Boyd.

Military officials, not pleased with the crowd's reaction, wanted a greater show of anger, more fervor. Cadre officers walked behind the crowds on each side of Trang Tien Street. They shouted, "We hate American people! Air pirates! Will be punish!"

Trucks drove up and down next to the procession. Under the bright glare of floodlights powered by a generator on a truck bed, military agitators verbally goaded the Americans. Mockeries and jeers began in earnest.

"Kill Jonshon. Kill MacMara!"

Marching sixth in line, Ron Byrne, his humor alive as he heard the increased verbal harangue, turned slightly left toward Larry Guarino.

"Right on cue. Perfect timing."

Past the intersection of Pho Ngo Quyen, previously named Rue Henri Riviere on which sat the Metropole Hotel, spectators became even more expressive. On the left came, "Decisively punish American air pirates who violate the skies over our capital."

Simultaneously from the other side, a screaming shout: "Americans no good."

The behind-the-scene military cheerleaders continued with simple, vitriolic rants.

"Americans go home. We not want you."

The Rabbit's bullhorn became more strident.

"Must show remorse! Must show shubmission!"

Multitudes of bystanders, standing beneath a concrete overhang supported by white columns, yelled in unison.

"Air creemeenals pay blood!"

Al Brudno and Bill Tschudy, now well along Trang Tien Street, maintained their countenance. *Nothing to worry about,* Tschudy reasoned. Concern began to set in, however, as the Americans looked farther down Trang Tien Street at the Vietnamese who, stepping off the curb, coalesced into a fuming, impenetrable mass. Forty people deep on both sides, the thick, boisterous crowd packed the sidewalks, spilling onto the street itself, obstructing the way forward.

Angry shouts increased as fists shot into the air. But if any sign of trepidation showed on the faces of Brudno and Tschudy, panic did not.

For Skip Brunhaver and Jerry Singleton, at twenty-first position, the parade thus far was relatively smooth. But Singleton, knowing this was only the start, had a foreboding feeling the evening would turn bad. He questioned whether the North Vietnamese officials could handle the seething turbulence lurking ahead. Since the prisoners were hobbled at the wrists, guards, each carrying an automatic weapon, would be able to control them. But could the guards really control the crowds? Singleton gained the sense neither he nor Brunhaver would survive the night.

Much shorter than the Americans, guards, their sleeves rolled up, kept their bayonet-tipped rifles pointed in toward the prisoners.

Jim Bell and Ralph Gaither, in twenty-fifth position, brought up the rear of the march sequence. Both men verbally and courageously expressed their personal convictions.

"Americans, stay strong!"

Just as Bell and Gaither were about to make the turn at the roundabout onto Trang Tien Street in front of the Hanoi Opera House, a man ran up to Bell and quickly smashed his face with a vicious roundhouse punch while at the same time yelling, "You millionaire son-of-a-bitch!"

The unexpected attack staggered Bell. Ralph Gaither steadied his partner so he could regain his balance and composure. With a bloody nose and a wry, contorted smile, Bell, stumbling slightly, made light of the back-handed compliment.

"Hear that? He just called me a millionaire."

If an American fell nearer the front or in the middle, others would be tripped up and fall, too, causing a precarious situation. The Vietnamese would be on them in seconds and cause serious harm. Some Americans, however, would benefit from safety in numbers.

On the other hand, if Bell and Gaither, who had fallen slightly behind, were to go down, there would be no other friendly person to help them. Their being last in line, isolated from their comrades in front, Bell and Gaither would be beaten to death in an instant.

The crowd gathered behind the two Americans, heckling them. Bell, still unsteady, with warm blood running down his neck, turned his head to observe what was happening, but was clubbed. Gaither, again holding him upright, didn't let him fall.

All twenty-five pairs of Americans, fifty men in all, were now formed on Trang Tien Street. The line, three hundred feet long, lengthened and shortened like an accordion.

At the front, Rabbit continued with the bullhorn.

"You show respect people Vietnam!"

The guards lumbered along the street next to the detested criminals while maintaining their vigilance. Military personnel exhorted the crowd's anger by shouting hateful invective They encouraged similar responses from the teeming masses.

Rabbit climbed out of the sidecar. He caught eye of Everett Alvarez and raised the bullhorn as he pointed.

"Alvarez! Alvarez! Son-of-a-bitch! Son-of-a-bitch!"

The crowd followed suit.

"Avrez, Avrez, sonbitch, sonbitch!"

Four positions behind Alvarez, Spot placed his hands on the top of Dick Ratzlaff's head to yank it down to a bowing position. Ratzlaff, paired with Bill Shankel, was so determined to resist, he almost lifted Spot's feet off the pavement.

Foreign photographers in front and often mingling among the

ranks of the sweating Americans, snapped hundreds of photos while officials, inciting the crowds, continued their loud growling.

Bob Purcell, convinced no one in the U.S. knew whether he was still alive, surmised if his image surfaced outside of Vietnam, the Vietnamese would be obliged to confirm he was held in Hanoi. Purcell looked straight into the cameras.

Porter Halyburton, marching to the right of Art Burer in sixteenth position, was certain, like Purcell, that people back home knew nothing of his fate. Perhaps any film or photo that caught him might find its way to the States. He, too, stared at the cameras.

The number 007 was crudely painted on the back of Alan Lurie's prison clothes. Lurie, tied to Darrel Pyle, just in front of Jim Bell and Ralph Gaither, thought for sure the number, synonymous with the James Bond movies in the U.S., would catch someone's attention and he would be recognized.

Smitty Harris, paired with Bob Shumaker nearer the front in fifth position, heard MiGs flying in circles overhead probably as a covering patrol. He looked up slightly into the black sky but all he could see were buildings not more than three stories high on each side of the street.

Howie Dunn and Ray Merritt, positioned at the front of the second group, at number fourteen, heard the Rabbit's incitements as he walked up and down the column and back and forth in front of them.

"Creemeenals! You bow!"

Merritt responded clearly, "We ain't bowing shit!"

"Got that right!" Dunn said.

A man in the crowd spoke in perfect English.

"Why do you come here to kill our people?"

Lights swept past Al Brudno and Bill Tschudy to focus on the bystanders. The Vietnamese, gesticulating wildly, went crazy.

The Rabbit noticed neither Bob Purcell nor Jon Reynolds obeyed his instructions. Enraged at such insubordination, Rabbit yelled louder into the bullhorn as he pointed at the two recalcitrant men.

"YOU BOW!"

A guard jumped on Purcell's back to shove his head down.
Purcell shrugged his body.

"Get off me, you bastard."

The guard fell away.

"You OK, Percy?" Reynolds asked.

Reynolds found humor in the incident. "What friends you have."

Purcell laughed.

"Hell of a football game, huh?"

Spit from the twisted mouths of angry onlookers, much of it polluted with juice from chewing beetle nut, was hurled at the prisoners from every angle. The gooey spittle, like endless, slanting sleet, was silver-white in the light against the contrast of the night. The prisoners' uniforms were wet from top to bottom due to their perspiration but also from the disgusting spit.

Near the back, a guard instructed Skip Brunhaver and Jerry Singleton to lower their heads which they didn't do. In a quick movement, the guard raised his rifle and swung the forestock hard into the back of Singleton's head. Brunhaver, who saw Singleton stumbling forward, reached his free left arm around his body to keep him upright.

Angry Vietnamese spectators had congregated at the intersection of Trang Tien and Hang Bai Streets, the most popular place where teenage boys, acting tough, gather for entertainment on Friday nights. The Americans moving on Trang Tien Street were approaching the craze-filled intersection.

The side streets acted as human conduits. Pressing onto Trang Tien Street, onlookers created a narrow passage through which the prisoners walked. The crowd grew increasingly restless and inched closer to the Americans. People yelled, "We want blood of creemeenal America men."

A single lightbulb suspended on wires attached to poles on opposite corners of the intersection, garishly illuminated Al Brudno and Bill Tschudy and the bedraggled Americans who followed.

American astronauts would not walk on the moon for three

more years. But now, at this moment, on the evening of 6 July 1966, fifty American airmen, escorted by armed guards, were being forced to walk not through a lunar desolation as part of an epoch scientific journey, but through shouting, threatening, unfamiliar crowds along a dismal street in downtown Hanoi in the darkness after sundown.

The American prisoners traversed a distance of one thousand four hundred feet. With the exception of a few heads forced down and airborne spit, the procession along Hanoi's Trang Tien Street, although raucous, was orderly.

What the Americans experienced on Hanoi's narrow main street, however, was just a forerunner of events that would soon unfold. The Americans were about to enter an endless, churning melee filled with delirium and madness.

The main entrance to Hoa Lo prison, ironically called the Hanoi Hilton, on Hoa Lo Street. Hoa Lo served as the main receiving center for captured American airmen. Upon their release in 1973, the American POWs emerged from these doors into freedom and were repatriated to the USA. The prison was one block from the march route. *Author's collection*

The Hanoi Opera House and plaza from which the Hanoi March began. The Americans were assembled in the area to the right of the Opera House. The building in the background is the Hilton Hotel built in 2000. *Author's collection*

The motorcycle traffic from left to right is on the same path the POWs followed around the traffic circle in 1966 at the start of the march. *Author's collection*

Trang Tien Street facing the Hanoi Opera House and looking in the opposite direction of the march. *Author's collection*

Still looking in the opposite direction of the march on Trang Tien Street. Photo shows typical buildings much the way they were in 1966. *Author's collection*

Hang Khay Street looking in the direction of the march. A large park and Hoan Kiem Lake are located just to the right. *Author's collection*

Present-day souvenir shops on Hang Khay Street. *Author's collection*

Trang Thi Street looking in direction of Hanoi March. The building to the right is the Hoan Kiem District Police Headquarters. *Author's collection*

THE HANOI MARCH

CHAPTER 20

INTO DARKNESS –
PHO HANG KHAY AND
PHO TRANG THI

The American lineup, shuffling along, crossed the big intersection with Pho Hang Bai and, slipping beneath its solitary light—the last of the light—progressed straight ahead into a darker chasm in a furious, chanting throng of people on Pho Hang Khay. The onlookers' attitude became bolder. Their demeanor changed.

Giant trees lining each side of the boulevard created a portentous atmosphere absorbing all light, casting the passageway into an abyss. Al Brudno and Bill Tschudy, and the following line of paired prisoners continued into the obscure tunnel beneath the tree limbs, thick with leaves, that shrouded the silhouettes of packed, churning people. The Americans disappeared into oblivion.

Makeshift grandstands gave way to thousands of people standing next to the street and off the curbs. Guards, their bayonets pointed dangerously at the prisoners, continued to walk to each side of the line. The entire entourage had difficulty passing through the thrashing crowd.

Everett Alvarez, tied to Robbie Risner, caught vague sight of a sign in the darkness advertising Seiko watches. It was hanging outside a shop on the left side.

Moving slowly, the Americans unknowingly passed immediately south of Hoan Kiem Lake, the sacred body of water with a quaint pagoda at the opposite end of the lake and another much smaller one in the middle. The lake was bounded by an open park to the right of the marchers. The Americans could not see the park or the lake due to thousands of people extending forever into the blackness.

The hidden park provided a sinister veil, an evil dwelling from which malevolence was promulgated with impunity. The absence of light beckoned the devils of night; and they answered the call.

Rabbit's redundancy continued. The bullhorn sounded again.

"Creemeenals, bow head!"

Defiant, Bill Tschudy, to the right of Al Brudno, did not do as the Rabbit instructed. He almost lost consciousness when a rifle butt smashed him from behind. A guard hit Tschudy's head a second time. Tschudy acquiesced only long enough to regain his senses.

Kile Berg, tied at the wrist with Pop Keirn, in the fourth slot, did not obey the instruction to keep his head down either. Berg paid for his insolence while taking hits to his face. A rifle butt crashed into the back of his skull.

Stunned by the impact, Berg managed to maintain his dignity and pride. He held his head up. A rifle butt pounded him again. Berg's eyes rolled to the top of his head as he stumbled. Pop Keirn, himself a target, grabbed Berg's arms and kept him from falling to the pavement.

The verbal nastiness of the Vietnamese, no longer enough, morphed into vile hysteria. Bolstered by the sight of other guards hitting the Americans with their rifles, hundreds of people brazenly perpetrated their own brand of punishment.

As the first American pairs proceeded well along Pho Hang Khay, farther back, Jerry Coffee and Art Cormier, marching in eighteenth position, approached the melee just past the intersection with Hang Bai Street. The wrist bindings tying the two men together came loose. Seeing this, young Vietnamese men tugged at the two prisoners. Both Americans, each depending on and helping the other, had to act in unison if they were to survive. They grabbed each other's hand and held on tightly as they struggled against the rioting Vietnamese who were trying to separate and beat them.

The attackers relinquished their grip. Coffee and Cormier staggered forward.

Simultaneously, farther on Pho Hang Khay, a man walked to the left of Bill Shankel and Dick Ratzlaff, in seventh position. He tried to pull them down while yelling at them.

"We kill you aggressor pirates and burn your bodies."

Shankel's response was quick and simple.

"Get lost, asshole."

The multitudes of people had completely blocked the way on Pho Hang Khay near Ba Trieu Street. The Americans, trying to find an opening, bunched up and stopped behind Al Brudno and Bill Tschudy.

Ev Alvarez, two positions behind, seeing the anger and realizing there was no room in which to maneuver, turned to his left.

"Robbie, we might not make it through this."

A small number of Vietnamese focused their fury on Risner and Alvarez and continued to harangue them, then slapped and hit them from every side.

Eight positions back, a mob of people descended on David Hatcher and Larry Spencer and brought the procession almost to a standstill. The Vietnamese accosted each man. They tried to pull their heads down. The two men resisted but could not avoid the multiple assaults.

Guards, with wide-eyed expressions of fear growing on their faces, didn't know how to handle this worsening scenario. Taking the lead from the officers, they stepped in and opened a passage through the crowd. With lots of yelling and use of rifle butts, they were able to push the crowd back a few feet to make a gap large enough for the pairs of prisoners to proceed.

Now, instead of pointing their bayonets toward the Americans, the guards began to slant them out toward the onlookers. However, the disorderly people didn't pay attention to the guards or their bayonets. Increasing their protests, the Vietnamese onlookers unashamedly and without fear, continued to move in among the ranks of the shuffling prisoners.

At the intersection with Pho Ba Trieu, a group of ten young men broke from the curb and, with clenched fists, raced past the guards toward the lead Americans. The pugnacious hoodlums hit and kicked Brudno and Tschudy and slapped at Phil Butler and Hayden Lockhart.

Farther back, onlookers from the sidelines hurled objects which sailed over the heads of Wendy Rivers and Duffy Hutton in tenth position.

A bottle of beer bounced off the top of Phil Butler's head. The impact stunned him as his vision quickly faded. Hayden Lockhart, standing to Butler's right in second position, helped him regain his balance and supported him using both his arms. Butler, his eyes glazed over, slumped. Lockhart held him tightly while they continued to walk. Butler mimicked Lockhart's gait to stay with him. Embarrassed by his ironic but spontaneous thought, Lockhart couldn't help but think: *What a waste of beer.*

In fourteenth position, leading the second group, Howie Dunn and Ray Merritt were hit by a handful of rocks that momentarily stunned them.

Airborne clutter fell among the marchers in front of Dunn and Merritt and hit Vietnamese bystanders on the opposite side of the street. Flying debris became so plentiful, Bob Purcell, eighth in line, turned to Jon Reynolds.

"We better put our heads down. Too much crap in the air."

The Rabbit, walking freely in and out and up and down the American column, circulated among the prisoners. He admonished the prisoners loudly and angrily.

"Show respect, creemeenals."

Cole Black and Chuck Boyd, at the end of the first group, and Howie Dunn and Ray Merritt, the first of the second group, and

Alan Brunstrom and Render Crayton, behind them, dodged fists and kicks but were clubbed in their heads.

Farther back yet, Vietnamese men and women hit any American they could, exacting any injury possible. Some guards attempted to stop them but were unable to exert any control. The bullhorn and the loud chants had accomplished their intended objective of stirring the people up.

Ed Davis and Jim Hivner, in twenty-second position, were kicked in their shins and slapped on the back of their heads.

Al Brudno and Bill Tschudy, at the front, worked through the blockage. Without knowing it, they crossed Pho Ba Trieu while continuing to march ahead of the others.

Phil Butler and Hayden Lockhart lost momentum and fell behind Brudno and Tschudy. The lineup stalled again. The more militant bystanders quickly descended on the unfortunate pair and beat the two men viciously.

Just behind, the same group of men who earlier attacked Robbie Risner and Everett Alvarez found them again and kicked and hit them hard. Risner fell to the pavement. Alvarez helped him up while being attacked. He dragged Risner forward.

A young man slipped into the ranks and gave Risner a hard Judo chop to the back of his neck. Risner lost his vision and was beginning to fade. Alvarez, unsteady, his head spinning, kept his mate from falling.

The two injured men trudged forward, each holding the other.

But as Risner staggered on, another assailant caught him under his chin with an uppercut that just about ripped his head from his shoulders. Again, Alvarez helped him as he warded off others who were attacking his injured mate.

"I'm still with you, Robbie," Alvarez said.

Three youths attacked Wes Schierman, marching with Ron Storz in twenty-third position and, yelling in his face, tried to rip his shirt off. Schierman lost his balance but Storz pulled him upright.

Guards, seeing the unruliness of the mobs, were visibly shaking with fear. They marched alongside the prisoners with bayonets now unmistakably pointed toward the crowd.

Enraged people continued to force themselves into the middle of the street. They surrounded Bruce Seeber and Rob Doremus, in nineteenth position, and Len Eastman and Paul Galanti, just behind, while continuously screaming and threatening their safety.

The Americans and Vietnamese onlookers were separated by inches. Spacing of the lead pairs became less as the column of prisoners passed through the intersection with Quang Trung Street. Now on Pho Trang Thi, the Americans continued to march through humid, squalid Hanoi in the darkness toward some unknown destination.

The airborne menace aimed at the Americans grew to include rotten vegetables and table scraps, chicken innards and animal bones. Spit sailed overhead. Garbage and a wet patina covered the pavement.

Alan Lurie and Darrel Pyle, in twenty-fourth position, incurred the rage of the Rabbit who was walking now near the end of the line. Perturbed by their disobeying his orders to bow, the Rabbit slapped each man hard. Rabbit and a couple of guards struggled to force Lurie and Pyle's heads down, but without success.

An East German man yelled at Larry Guarino and Ron Byrne, nearer the front in sixth position.

"You'll be executed, you son-of-a-bitch imperialist shit pig!"

Guarino, a tough Italian who experienced his share of action in World War II and Korea, was not having any of this diatribe. He stared coldly at the man.

"Go screw yourself."

Ron Byrne smiled slightly and chuckled as he had before at Guarino's remark. But then, an incredible thing happened. Byrne could not believe his eyes.

Smitty Harris and Bob Shumaker, in fifth position, marched directly in front of Guarino and Byrne. A woman standing at the edge of the crowd just on the outside of the guards threw her son, not more than five years old, over the picket line. The boy landed on Harris. The small boy's arms and fists flailed at Harris until he shook him off. The child fell to the pavement and dashed through the guards to safety.

At the back of the first group, Cole Black and Chuck Boyd, helping each other, struggled through a small mob that had descended on them. Cole Black was kicked in his knees.

Jerry Coffee, at eighteenth position, just before Quang Trung Street, felt his sandals slipping from his feet. He began hobbling along to try to reposition them on each foot, but he was losing pace. Debris on the pavement cut his feet. Art Cormier, Coffee's partner, spoke up quickly.

"Keep walking, Jerry. If we stop, damn, they'll kill us for sure."

Back at the front, Hayden Lockhart, to the right of Phil Butler, was attacked. A young girl came through the ranks. Her eyes were full of anger. Butler, his head throbbing from the earlier bottle impact, saw her and yelled, "Hayden, look out!"

Lockhart's reaction wasn't fast enough. The girl hit him squarely in the jaw.

In a separate attack, a woman broke from the curb with a broom and hit Lockhart in the nose and eyes with the handle. His broken nose and cheek were bleeding.

Well beyond Phu Duan Street, both Butler and Lockhart were staggering like puppets.

The Vietnamese had gone completely berserk.

If the U.S. airmen were going to their deaths, it would be more likely at the hands of rioting, out-of-control citizens, not through a government procedure, real or fake. The Americans' lives depended on the guards. But the guards, acting more nervous, were searching for a way out.

Alan Lurie, second from last, gained some respite. He looked to his right to gauge his surroundings. Surprised by a sudden sharp slap to his head, Lurie almost fell down. Darrel Pyle, Lurie's mate, caught a heavy slap, too, straight to his face.

While Jim Bell and Ralph Gaither, struggling through the fracas near Phu Duan Street, brought up the rear, Al Brudno and Bill Tschudy, in the lead on Pho Trang Thi, would soon cross Quan Su Street. If the march turned left, the Americans would soon arrive at Hoa Lo prison, but the march continued straight.

Frightening so far, the brutality was just getting started.

CHAPTER 21

HALFWAY — NGA NAM

The column of Americans, moving slowly through the streets of Hanoi, undulated like a long, heaving dragon with a life of its own. The march was impeded at times. As if on a conveyor belt, the airmen stacked up.

Al Brudno and Bill Tschudy could anticipate what was happening in front, but could only surmise events occurring behind them. Those who followed never knew what was coming next. At the tail end of the line, Jim Bell and Ralph Gaither had a more compelling concern: Not what was ahead but what was behind.

Waves of physical retribution from the onlookers swept up and down the line, subsiding here and erupting there. Even when there might be moments of calm in the middle, each end of the parade received continuous onslaughts and vice-a-versa. The insanity Brudno and Tschudy experienced would dissipate only to resurface somewhere along the line as the destructive onlookers moved on to their next victims. The ugliness didn't stop.

Having covered four thousand nine hundred feet, Al Brudno and Bill Tschudy and forty-eight airmen behind them approached a curiosity.

Created by generations, if not centuries of crisscrossing paths and cart trails, confusing roads converged in a small area. Businesses on the ground floor created a tight congestion of foot and vehicle traffic intermingling within the web of this corner of Hanoi. Owners and tenants living above in narrow quarters on the second and third floors had a bird's eye view of ensuing activities, not more than five feet from the shops' doors directly below their windows. Lanterns, casting a pallor on the scene below, sat on the ledges of the laundry-draped balconies.

While others far behind were crossing Quan Su Street, Al Brudno and Bill Tschudy were leading the column of Americans, some with serious injuries, into Hanoi's famed five-way intersection. It was called Nga Nam.

Overflowing with humanity, Nga Nam was packed with thousands of overwrought people all calling for American blood. The agitated, angry throng completely filled the narrow streets and walkways, blocking store fronts and, more importantly, the way forward for the Americans.

Two cable cars from Cau Giay arrived not far away. The passengers flooded toward Nga Nam to have a clearer look at the faces of the American pilots, people they had never before seen.

The masses, berating and shouting, surrounded and infiltrated the column of Americans from every side street. Crazed bystanders grabbed their shirts so tightly many Americans stumbled. Some were taken down. At the front, onlookers beat and kicked Brudno and Tschudy while demanding they be punished in a manner appropriate to their crimes.

"Death now! Blood for blood!"

Order was deteriorating. The guards, so fearful, not knowing what action to take, were ineffective with crowd control. Now in the tightness of Nga Nam, the Americans' safety was in serious question, their lives in doubt. Still, the best defense, the only option, was to just keep going.

In seventh position, Bill Shankel, tied to Dick Ratzlaff, in the middle of the first group, thought he recognized some bystanders in the riotous crowd he had seen earlier. He realized the mob was following the Americans and contributed to the bunching, congestion and chaos.

JB McKamey, in ninth position, kept hearing the annoying, oft-repeated bowing command and knew what the results would be if he didn't lower his head. McKamey took no heed.

"We're not bowing our heads," McKamey said, reiterating Paul Kari's earlier statement.

McKamey felt the flat of a guard's bayonet on the back of his neck.

McKamey was clobbered in the face by a woman wielding a high-heel shoe. The candid thought crossed McKamey's mind as he reacted in agony: *Where'd she find that?*

A small woman walked alongside the marchers but behind Jerry Denton and Bob Peel, located in twelfth position. She was carrying a hat filled with rocks the size of small oranges. While she threw several rocks at Denton, none hit its mark with serious impact. But then, a good-size rock found Denton's head, stunning him to the point he fell. He dragged Peel down with him. Denton's vision went temporarily blank. His ears immediately filled with a loud ringing, rushing sound.

Peel stood up to a crouch and steadied Denton back on his feet. Just then, a short Vietnamese man leapt from the mass of humanity on the sideline and punched Denton in his groin. Denton was temporarily immobilized. Peel helped him regain his balance.

Render Crayton, to the right of Alan Brunstrom, in fifteenth slot, was attacked by a woman who hit him hard in the back of the head with a solid object. Stunned, Crayton staggered on as Brunstrom steadied him. Not more than twenty feet later, a man kicked Crayton in the stomach, immediately knocking the air out of him. He stayed standing with Brunstrom's help. Crayton, moaning, regained his breath.

A man walking to Art Cormier's right and slightly ahead wielded a bamboo pole. He followed Jerry Driscoll, in front of Cormier, until he could affect a good swing. At the right moment, the man raised the bamboo stick and swung it hard. Cormier heard the swish as the stick cut through the air and the whack as it struck Driscoll in the head.

In back of Jerry Coffee and Cormier, Bruce Seeber and Rob Doremus, occupying the nineteenth slot, were spat upon, hit and repeatedly kicked. They tried to dodge the shower of bottles, food and rocks. A few of the projectiles hit the two men.

"Look, there's *Xi-bo*," a woman cried. "*May chet!*" ("You die!")

Another woman kicked at Seeber and Doremus while screaming.

"I am not afraid of you! You criminals! No good!"

Others reached out and grabbed the two airmen and yanked on them, making them almost fall.

The wave of loathing intensified. The mob pressed in. There was no room to move. The Vietnamese became more compressed and more physical. Nga Nam was consuming the Americans one by one.

Paul Galanti, to the right of Leonard Eastman, at the back in twentieth position behind Seeber and Doremus, was startled to see a man appear from the thick mass. His fists were doubled up to strike but instead he used his feet. The man delivered a solid, straight-forward soccer kick to Galanti's groin. Galanti collapsed in a heap. Eastman pulled him up.

Ed Davis with Jim Hivner on his right in twenty-second position, was struck in the face, then clobbered on the back of his head. Davis was spinning. The wounds bled instantly. Davis, faltering, was barely able to stand. He stumbled forward. Jim Hivner, also sustaining numerous hits, spoke supportively to Davis while tugging him back to his feet: "Got to hold on, Ed."

The angry crowd, sensing the two prisoners were in trouble, descended on both men. They set upon yanking Hivner away from Davis. Still feeling the effects of his earlier beating, Davis saw what was happening and pulled Hivner back in line. The attacks didn't stop, but Davis and Hivner, although stunned, made it through the crisis and were again walking in step with the other Americans.

The pairs far in front of Jim Bell and Ralph Gaither disappeared from view. Bell and Gaither, at the very back, caught sight of Ron Storz and Wes Schierman and Alan Lurie and Darrel Pyle, just ahead, fending off attackers. Bell and Gaither followed them and were also caught in the middle of Nga Nam's chaos with no escape possible. They were hit with sticks as people attacked them from all sides.

Jim Bell and Ralph Gaither, as did others before them, would survive the last of the anarchy of the five-way intersection. But in so doing, Bell and Gaither did something they would do again. They fought back.

THE HANOI MARCH

CHAPTER 22

THE LONGEST STRETCH – PHO NGUYEN THAI HOC

N ow, with the last of the American lineup through Nga Nam, little did Jim Bell or Ralph Gaither or any American in front of them know what was about to transpire.

Just beyond Nga Nam, North Vietnam's north-south railway intersected the march route at an angle on Pho Nguyen Thai Hoc. The rail line would demark American-designated Route Packages 6A and 6B, the separation for U.S. Air Force and Navy air operations.

Trains, with their thunderous, throbbing sound and punctuating whistle, along with the clamorous, rickety tracks beneath, cut like a chainsaw right along the eastern edge of Hanoi's Ba Dinh District, in a densely populated part of the city. People lived, ate and slept in their homes on both sides of the tracks, in a slit of a canyon between dwellings. The buildings, just feet from the tracks, would shake when the loud, hulking trains passed.

The mobs of Nga Nam followed the Americans now on Pho Nguyen Thai Hoc. Young men in small gangs harassed and taunted the airmen. In the lead, Al Brudno and Bill Tschudy, deflecting those attackers, stumbled across the tracks and continued marching toward the west. Three teenage boys, mocking the prisoners and pulling their hair, threw rocks at Brudno and Tschudy, then prodded and hit them with long sticks.

Phil Butler and Hayden Lockhart remained a focus of Vietnamese attackers as the people continuously slugged and kicked each American.

While Cuban interest in the American prisoners was no secret, Cubans seized on the moment to shamelessly promote their menacing presence. They had walked alongside Everett Alvarez, taunting him constantly in Spanish. They stepped up their outbursts and began taking hard swings at the young American from California. They shouted.

"*Hijo de puta!*" ("Son-of-a-bitch!") "*Hijo de puta!*"

A sweating, shirtless man emerged from nowhere and goaded Alvarez.

"Criminal must pay now blood."

Farther on, another man cursed at Alvarez while aggressively pacing him. Not satisfied with the American's reaction, the man removed his camera and, using it as a bludgeon, struck Alvarez in the back of his head.

Alvarez sank to his knees.

Robbie Risner, on the left, stooped to help Alvarez regain his balance.

Just behind, Pop Keirn received a hard shock to his head by some object and fell down. Kile Berg, still feeling the earlier pain from a rifle butt, reached down and pulled Keirn back to his feet. Berg and Keirn leaned against each other for support as they stumbled along.

Jon Reynolds and Bob Purcell, in eighth position, crossed the tracks while dodging teenagers who tried to kick them.

Duffy Hutton, to the right of Wendy Rivers in tenth position, dodged some of the attackers, but there were too many of them. Hutton's face, the receiving end of many fists, turned deep purple and black. The swelling caused one eye to close.

At the same time, to the left of Hutton, a man swiftly kicked Wendy Rivers with all his might in the groin. Rivers, immobilized, bent over and fell to the pavement. The crowd went wild with screaming taunts. Hutton, his vision impaired and his own face bleeding, paid no mind to the loud pandemonium or risks to himself. He pulled Rivers up and helped him stay on his feet.

"We'll make it, Wendy. We'll get through this, pardner."

As Al Brudno and Bill Tschudy marched beyond Le Duan Street, a Vietnamese man running the length of the American line toward the rear passed Jon Reynolds and Bob Purcell and, striking Wendy Rivers and Duffy Hutton and David Hatcher and Larry Spencer, eyed Jeremiah Denton in twelfth position just at the railroad tracks. Denton recognized him as his earlier attacker.

The man kicked Denton solidly in the groin. Denton, still aching from previous attacks, immediately doubled up as nausea consumed him. Once again Peel helped him back to his feet.

"Stay with me, commander."

The North Vietnamese man persisted. He tried again several times in rapid succession, but without hitting his target directly.

Denton and Peel, knowing the man would attack them again, practiced coordinating an uppercut motion with their tied hands. Also, remembering the power of a short punch if one lays one's shoulder and weight into it, what Denton casually referred to as a six-inch punch, Denton demonstrated to Bob Peel with his free hand how they should protect themselves.

"If that asshole does that again . . ."

But Denton's intentions toward his attacker extended beyond self-protection. "Let's give the bastard his due."

Having crossed the railroad tracks and approaching Le Duan Street with the leaders far ahead, Denton and Peel, preparing for another assault, perfected their punches. A soldier they recognized as Spot gazed at them curiously.

Denton indicated to Spot what he and Bob Peel were intending to do. Through an exaggerated stomping action, Denton demonstrated the attacker's head would be flattened into the pavement and ground under foot.

His eyes following the attacker, Denton gestured directly at the young thug. The message was clear: If you continue your crap, my little friend, you're gonna meet with an uncomfortable fate.

"Come on, buddy," Denton said. "Try again."

Convinced of his invincibility and fueled by agitated hatred, the attacker rushed at Denton one more time to assault him and Bob Peel.

Spot, who saw Denton and Peel practicing their movements, withdrew his pistol from its holster and immediately smashed the man's face. The Vietnamese tormentor, reeling from the pistol's hard impact, with blood streaming from his nose and a gash on his face, scurried away into the mass of people.

From the side, a woman sprang at Cole Black, next to Chuck Boyd, at the last of the first group, and grabbed his arm to pull him out of line. Black lost his sandals and his balance. He stumbled as he was hit in the mouth. Blood ran down his neck and shirt.

Fifteen seconds later, a man with a bamboo pole, perhaps the same man who struck Jerry Driscoll, approached Chuck Boyd and swung it. The stick hit its target. Stunned, Boyd moaned in agony as he covered his face with his free hand.

Nearer the front before Hoang Dieu Street, in the pervasive chaos and wildness of the crowd, Groucho, a Zoo turnkey, warned a guard behind him to be careful with his bayonet. The guard didn't pay attention and continued on carelessly. When the procession became jammed, he inadvertently stabbed Groucho in his backside. Groucho turned around and slapped the guard hard.

Ron Storz and Wes Schierman, handcuffed next to each other in twenty-third position, at the back of the pack, dodged various attacks. Storz, being the taller, was the more accessible target and took most of the blows dished out by the North Vietnamese.

A woman not five feet high reached up and hit Ron Storz in the face with her wood shoe. Storz staggered for a moment. His nose, bleeding freely, was broken. Wes Schierman kept him upright on his feet. Schierman's arms were covered with blood gushing from Storz's injury.

To the left of Skip Brunhaver, marching to the left of Jerry Single-ton, ahead of Storz and Schierman, a man spoke in perfect English.

"You! ... Must! ... Show! ... Respect!"

Spectators ran into the ranks and savagely attacked Brunhaver and Singleton. Brunhaver was hit numerous times in the face and back of the head. His shirt was tugged almost from his body.

Three positions ahead, a wood shoe careened off Art Cormier's head and flew toward the curb while bottles shattered on the pavement.

"Son-of-a-bitch!" Cormier yelled as he felt the back of his head. "Goddamnit!"

A moment later, a woman ran through the guards and hit Cormier hard in the stomach.

"Holy crap!" Cormier said, as he struggled to regain his breath. "Can you believe this shit?"

The same woman grabbed Cormier and started to pull him down. Jerry Coffee turned and, fending off the woman, lifted Cormier up. Cormier regained his feet.

A short man caught Coffee with a wild punch thrown at maximum force right to his face splitting both his lips. Blood flowed from Coffee's mouth like tomato juice pouring out of an open can. Coffee's damaged teeth were knocked loose.

Not a minute later, another woman hit Cormier hard in the face with the point of her conical peasant hat, causing his nose to bleed.

Several North Koreans, having finished their evening meal, ventured around the corner from their embassy and stood on the sidewalk of Pho Nguyen Thai Hoc just west of Hoang Dieu Street. Composed, they observed the mayhem before returning to their embassy. A Korean official yelled back, "Down with the invading American aggressors!"

At the front, the lead pairs made their way toward Van Mieu Street. Insanity, now a common phenomenon, continued.

Hand tools including screwdrivers and hammers littered the

street beneath the feet of the marchers. They had obviously been thrown at the American airmen.

Vietnamese men, their teeth darkly stained from tobacco, were thrusting their hands into the air.

"We don't want American pirates!"

Women, their teeth equally discolored from chewing beetle nut, yelled louder and flailed their fists.

"We kill you!"

Military agitators, walking along with the Americans but through the crowd, continued to spew hatred and anger to inflame the onlookers.

Far back, Jim Bell and Ralph Gaither, now across the railroad tracks and Pho Le Duan, walking toward the intersection with Hoang Dieu Street, brought up the rear. The brutality stepped up a notch. Both men were struck continuously. The men received cuts to their faces from women who dared to hit them with their shoes before quickly retreating. The women, more malicious than the men, isolated Bell and Gaither to pull them out of line, but the two men struggled to maintain their position.

Ray Merritt, to the right of Howie Dunn, was hit a glancing blow to his head by a rifle butt. He staggered but stayed upright and continued to march. His head was hit so often by rifle butts, it was throbbing.

Tom Barrett, in position seventeen behind Art Burer and Porter Halyburton, staggered when something hit his head. Jerry Driscoll slowed his walk enough to help Barrett regain his balance. The two continued to walk through the deafening noise and the melee of attackers while ducking airborne debris.

Farther on, two men broke through the cordon of guards and kicked Tom Barrett hard. He went down on one knee. Driscoll pulled him back up.

"Tom, we've gotta keep going. Can't stop now."

At the front, Al Brudno and Bill Tschudy, having crossed Van Mieu Street, were assaulted by an old woman wielding her cane.

From the other side, another much younger woman, her face angrily contorted while shouting, darted into the lineup on Pho Nguyen Thai Hoc. "American pigs you!" she screamed.

She started hitting Ron Byrne, marching to the right of Larry Guarino. A Vietnamese officer hit her hard with his fist and screamed at her to move away. She ran, leaving her shoes on the pavement.

Farther on, Byrne was told to keep his head low with the by-now overly-used refrain to bow. Reinforced by Jerry Denton's earlier instructions, Byrne was not going to give in to that idea.

A young, scrawny man sprang from the crowd and jumped on Byrne. The man tried to pull Byrne's head down with his hands placed around the back of his head without success. Byrne fought with the squirming attacker until the man finally gave up and retreated into the dark surroundings.

The last of the Americans, starting with Bruce Seeber and Rob Doremus, continued through the intersection with Pho Van Mieu. The assaults continued as each man deflected kicks and punches.

Near the front at Duc Thang Street, young girls and boys wearing white scouting-type shirts and red armbands swooped in on both sides of the Americans. They began floating in and out of the ranks exhibiting a holiday spirit while they held hands. They walked and danced within the column of Americans as the march proceeded. The teenagers formed a human chain between the onlookers and the walking prisoners. They seemed to be protecting the airmen. The guards were incapable of protecting anyone.

Al Brudno and Bill Tschudy approached Hang Vuong Street. They had walked eight thousand two hundred feet, about a mile and a half. Farther on, they were directed left off Pho Nguyen Tai Hoc.

The last leg of the march, still in front of them, covered a short distance, but the horror awaiting the prisoners wasn't close to being finished. Unimaginable ferocity was about to explode upon the long line of luckless Americans.

The worst lay ahead.

THE HANOI MARCH

CHAPTER 23

SANCTUARY – SAN VAN DONG HANG DAY

The column of disheveled Americans was well through the absurdities that occurred on Trang Tien, Hang Khay and Trang Thi Streets. The airmen weathered the madness at Nga Nam and, more recently, the fury along Pho Nguyen Thai Hoc. Now, they neared San Van Dong Hang Day (Hang Day Stadium), the same venue at which the prisoners from Briar Patch first arrived prior to assembly at the opera house plaza.

Bewildered by previous attacks, the American prisoners maintained their composure. But unable to predict what would emerge, anxiousness registered on their faces.

Organization and control of the march completely broke down. Neither the American prisoners nor the Vietnamese officials were psychologically prepared for the total collapse of order or the wicked group-think consuming the vengeful onlookers. Obviously frightened, the march officials didn't know what to do. The guards began to slink away, leaving the Americans to fend for themselves.

The way was open for agitated onlookers to exact their last and most brutal reprisal on their enemy.

The corridor through which the Americans were to walk disappeared altogether as the prisoners approached the stadium. A foaming mass of mad, hostile humanity greeted them.

The Americans continued to protect themselves from punching fists and kicking feet, but now with a difference: They fought back to save their very lives.

Painted green, a large wood gate allowed sports fans to pass into the stadium. It was through this gate that the bound American prisoners could gain safety, or so they would hope. It was the only way.

However, the gate swung out into the burgeoning crowd. With hundreds of people against the gate on the outside, pushing it open toward them from the other side would be almost impossible.

The Americans courageously confronted the angry mob raging in front of them. The hateful cheers, yelling and turbulence became magnified.

"Death to the Americans. We demand death!"

The earsplitting noise was at an all-time high pitch.

Neither Al Brudno nor his partner Bill Tschudy could see much ahead. Continuous shouting and ubiquitous commotion filled their ears. There being no discernable route forward, except through a wall of humanity, the two men now sensed the march was coming to an end, but what the end portended was unclear.

Brudno and Tschudy, as at Nga Nam, pushed into the demented mass. The thrashing, yelling mob didn't wait to mete out their hatred.

The North Vietnamese kicked at Brudno and Tschudy who, slowly making their way inch-by-inch through the crowd, returned the kicks in self-defense. The two prisoners sustained multiple hits, but both airmen, clenching their free fists, punched back at their assailants.

The gate, forced slightly but tenuously open from the inside, gave the two Americans optimism.

Brudno was first, then he pulled Tschudy. Their wrists were stinging from the tightness of their handcuffs. The strain placed on each man's arm was overwhelming. Somehow and with a lot of luck, they gave slip to the last of the attackers and made it through the opening. Brudno and Tschudy, both breathing heavily, were off the streets of Hanoi.

Out of harm's way, in a personal moment, escaping the carnage with fleeting touristic thoughts that would never be realized, Bill Tschudy, having seen a slice of Hanoi, reckoned it would be interesting during friendlier times to see neighborhoods, shops, houses and the city's residents going about their daily lives. Surely, Hanoi must possess at least one redeeming attribute. But what Tschudy saw on the evening of 6 July was shocking. The city, almost medieval in character, falling into a state of irreversible decline, seemed to be sinking into the quagmire of the Red River delta. The night air smelled of decay and swamp gas.

The noise at the gate behind the first two Americans woke Tschudy from his momentary thoughts to a new reality: The other Americans who marched behind were locked out. Brudno and Tschudy understood the implication. Their comrades won't survive!

Outside, the hysterical crowd, reacting to the lost opportunity due to the disappearance of Brudno and Tschudy, closed in completely on the remaining captives. The mad throng brought the procession to a halt. People, cursing loudly, their fists waving and swinging, intermingled with the hated Americans stranded at the closed gate. Any sense of protection for the prisoners vanished. The marchers behind the first pair became immediate targets of the crowd's supercharged wrath.

Phil Butler and Hayden Lockhart proceeded through the brawl.

From inside, the gate was being forced out into the crowd. A crack appeared, then the gate eased slightly more open.

Phil Butler, suffering from blows he received along the route, thought he would pass out at any moment.

"Steady, Phil," Lockhart said while being attacked.

Robbie Risner, Everett Alvarez, Kile Berg, Pop Keirn, Smitty Harris and Bob Shumaker, well bunched up, followed behind Butler and Lockhart. They faced fifty difficult feet before they would be out of harm's way.

Tumultuous madness swallowed Butler and Lockhart and the three pairs behind them.

A North Vietnamese soldier, his arms waving toward the gate-opening, hollered at the prisoners.

"GO!"

But with the dense fracas in front, moving with the same urgency as the instruction implied was impossible.

The soldier spoke again in an anxious voice, clearly indicating danger.

"RUN!"

Phil Butler's sandals fell off his feet, which were now sliding on the damp street. He dodged the broken glass on the pavement while stumbling over debris. A woman grabbed his hair and pulled it hard, abruptly yanking his head.

Butler and Lockhart struggled through the mass of sweating bodies and took hold of the edge of the gate to keep it open. They slipped through.

Just then, Ev Alvarez, immediately behind, was stunned by a sharp thump on the back of his head. Keeping his wits, Alvarez pressed on with Robbie Risner. Both Americans, fiercely fighting off their attackers, stepped through the opening.

Risner and Alvarez collapsed on the grass next to the running track. They were in a daze as to what had transpired.

Pop Keirn was hit on the head by an object. Kile Berg, stopped for a second and helped him with his balance. A lone guard urged them forward to the gate. Berg continued to steady Keirn as the two men slogged through the melee.

Berg spoke quickly: "Come on, Pop, we've gotta get in."

With one long push, Pop Keirn and Kile Berg made it inside the stadium.

The mob was ready and intending to do damage to the remaining Americans, starting with Smitty Harris and Bob Shumaker. The two pilots fought the Vietnamese with kicks and arm-pushing while making their way forward. Hands reached out to grab the men as they pushed back. Their clothes were almost ripped to shreds. Not enough, the Vietnamese pulled on their hair and kicked them, but could not stop their entrance into the stadium grounds.

Smitty Harris, still breathing hard, turned to his mate.

"Bob, think they'll make us do this again?"

The first five pairs, ten prisoners in all, had entered the gate sequentially none too soon. It immediately closed.

Outside the gate, wild Vietnamese pushed into the remaining marchers. The people closed up tightly like the neck of a funnel. Grubby hands reached out to grab the clothes of each prisoner to bring him down. Larry Guarino and Ron Byrne were being pulled apart by several young men. With a cynical sneer, Guarino turned to his partner. "Ain't this hell?"

For Guarino and Byrne, seeing what they had to do, as had others before them, passing through the gate was going to be problematic. The crowd was so dense and ferocious, the airmen's future was not looking good

"Look, it's creemeenal Greeno!" a woman yelled.

Larry Guarino was singled out. Like angry killer bees, the attackers, now sensing they were losing the opportunity to harm, even kill the hated Americans, lunged at Guarino who, slugging with his free hand, defended himself. Ron Byrne was right there in the fight as well. The two aviators, swinging their fists, worked their way through the frenetic mob toward the gate.

Inside, soldiers were trying to force the gate open. Slowly, it rotated outward on its hinges and revealed the promise of safety through a narrow gap.

A sole, terrified guard who remained on the sidelines urged the men to move faster. The lone guard wanted the prisoners to enter the gate if for no other reason than to save his own life.

"Let's run for it, Larry!" Byrne said. "This is it!"

With attackers now on the two Americans' backs, the bulk of flesh was too great to pass through the opening. One by one, the attackers fell away as Guarino and Byrne slithered through. Ron Byrne was first. He pulled Larry Guarino with him while Vietnamese pulled him back. The tug-of-war almost separated Guarino's arm from his shoulder. Guarino and Byrne's tied arms were stretched and twisted to the limit. Guarino's pain was excruciating. His right arm was burning.

Bill Shankel and Dick Ratzlaff, immediately behind Guarino and Byrne, confronted the same mob. The muddled scene was filled with swirling dust and frantic people waving arms and sticks and throwing debris. Shankel and Ratzlaff were determined not to let their lives end. They pushed forward. Shankel fell. Ratzlaff helped him up.

The mob yelled, kicked and hit at Shankel and Ratzlaff as they stumbled over a pile of bodies toward the gate. A soldier grabbed Shankel's shirt and dragged him and Ratzlaff through the opening.

Jon Reynolds, marching with Bob Purcell in eighth position, was anxious but never feared for his life during the march until at the gate to the stadium. Reynolds didn't think he or Purcell would survive.

A moving target is hard to hit, or so goes the theory. During the march, the targets were in motion, albeit slowly, but at the gate, the Americans were stopped, a perfect opportunity for the North Vietnamese to vent their hatred and manifest their anger. They didn't hesitate.

Reynolds and Purcell were able somewhat to protect their heads during the march but not at the gate. Looking out for each other as they took their lumps, each man fought the swarming mass and, together, using the last of their strength, scraped through the opening.

JB McKamey, to the left of Paul Kari, just behind Reynolds and Purcell, saw a young North Vietnamese soldier stumble and fall. McKamey, extending his free left hand, reached down and helped the soldier back to his feet.

Seconds later, a woman grabbed a handful of McKamey's hair

and yanked it out. Even with all the noise, others heard McKamey's hair being ripped from his scalp.

McKamey and Kari struggled toward the gate and in a quick maneuver, slid through the opening.

The number of marchers from whom the North Vietnamese could exact their revenge was finite. As each American pair entered the stadium, fewer and fewer targets would be available. Time was running out. The hate-filled North Vietnamese onlookers would not have another chance to punish the Americans.

Wendy Rivers and Duffy Hutton were caught by the mob and pummeled almost to the pavement, but they kept going and barely slid past the gate.

David Hatcher and Larry Spencer, at eleventh position, near the rear of the first group, followed their compatriots in front and, fighting through the crazed Vietnamese, approached the entrance. The night and the dust kicked up by the people obscured each man's vision while a clamor of strident voices and other noise filled the air.

To Larry Spencer, the emotional and physical madness roiled like a tempestuous storm across the rolling plains of his native Iowa. He and Hatcher received hits from rocks and shoes being wielded by women who screamed at the top of their lungs.

"*My chet!*" ("Death to Americans!")

At the gate opening, Hatcher and Spencer pulled each other through.

The shrieking swarm had grown to the point that Americans and the riotous bystanders were jumbled together with some spectators being knocked to the ground.

Jerry Denton and Bob Peel were right behind Hatcher and Spencer. The two Americans, who earlier had plotted their revenge with short punches against a man who kept attacking them, put their heads down as if on a football field and bullied forward. Like a big truck in its lowest gear, Denton and Peel gained momentum and, pushing and pulling, managed to gain the opening.

Cole Black and Chuck Boyd, thirteenth in the line-up, the last of the first group, struggled for the door. Black, barefoot, his mouth still bleeding, was suffering from the many hits he had received earlier forcing him to the pavement. Boyd, being vigilant to monitor his tethered mate, continued to give him support.

Black and Boyd, their free fists swinging, plunged straight forward through wailing, riotous Vietnamese. One by one, the two men, with bleeding arms, burning wrists and bursting lungs, made it inside.

Black who was shot down two weeks before and unfamiliar with prison routines and with blood now dripping from his chin onto his shirt, inquired of Boyd, "Do the Vietnamese do this often?

Chuck Boyd smiled ironically at Black's candid question.

"Only on Wednesdays."

Fifty percent of the prisoners made it through the gate at Hang Day Stadium. But fifty percent, fighting their way to the gate, remained outside. Through their own efforts, certainly not those of the North Vietnamese guards and officials, could the remaining Americans save their lives.

Howie Dunn and Ray Merritt, at number fourteen, led the second group. The gate loomed closer. Just before gaining access to the opening, a man carrying a briefcase emerged from the horde. He quickly approached Merritt from his right and swung the briefcase catching Merritt on the chin. The impact staggered Merritt. He would have fallen had it not been for Dunn who caught him.

Something hard, probably the briefcase again, slammed into the back of Merritt's head rendering him almost unconscious. The world around him whirled. Merritt's eyes became blurred. Stars congregated and exploded inside his head. Merritt tumbled forward but Dunn steadied him.

Howie Dunn, the only United States Marine in the march, placed Ray Merritt's life before his own. With a big forceful push, Dunn shoved Merritt through the gate first, then immediately followed him. Bleeding, his eyes rolling, Ray Merritt fell to his knees.

Outside, young Vietnamese continued to stumble, forming a bigger pile of humanity.

The cry and noise of the tumultuous crowd outside rose to in-credible heights as fists and sticks were waved in the air and debris sailed overhead.

People yelled and screamed in Vietnamese and English. While the meaning of the Vietnamese language could be guessed from the tone, the English resonated clearly.

"We hate you Americans! You not go home! We want you die! We bury you here!"

A voice coming from within the American ranks foretold the next logical phase.

"They're going to kill us now."

In another push, Alan Brunstrom and Render Crayton drew closer to the stadium right behind Dunn and Merritt. The Viet-namese, so close they were touching body to body, pressed for-ward and squeezed in on them. The Vietnamese spat directly into the faces of the two Americans while swinging their fists.

Brunstrom and Crayton fought with the attackers and climbed over the wriggling pile of bodies. In a quick instant, as the gate began to close, Brunstrom and Crayton passed through the narrow slit of the opening. Completely out of breath, the two men fell to the ground.

Inside the stadium, people screamed from the stands.

"Kill Mcmara! Kill Jone-shaun!"

Shaking their fists, the spectators raised their voices more. "Kill Washtin!"

Brunstrom laughed, his keen sense of humor undampened.

"Listen to those idiots. They think ole George is still alive."

Arthur Burer and Porter Halyburton, sixteenth in line, contin-ued toward the stadium. On the left and in front of them, Haly-burton saw the body of a young girl lying face-down in the street at the edge of the pile of trampled human beings. Her skin was a ghostly white. Her head, covered by long black hair, didn't move. People just walked over her.

Burer and Halyburton, both bleeding, were punched, hit and kicked but they punched, hit and kicked right back. They made it through the clamoring crowd over the bodies and entered the gate.

Tom Barrett and Jerry Driscoll could not push through. They fought against a large number of Vietnamese as they edged closer to the half-open gate. Surprisingly, a North Vietnamese army officer extended his hand to Driscoll who grabbed it. Together, each pulled the other. Driscoll climbed over the bodies and passed through the opening. He pulled Tom Barrett up and over the pile of people and also through the gate with his other hand which was tied to Barrett's. As he fought through the mountain of flesh, Barrett was convinced an American had been killed and was at the bottom.

The North Vietnamese onlookers outside the stadium were trying to keep the officials from opening the gate. They didn't want the remaining Americans gaining access to safety lest the rioters be denied the opportunity to exact their revenge.

The crowd pounced on Jerry Coffee, his lips still pouring blood from a previous attack. Both he and Art Cormier lashed out to protect themselves.

Another young girl had fallen. Jerry Coffee, now drenched in his own blood, helped her up by grabbing her arm. He hobbled along with her to a point where he thought she would be safe and let her go. Just then, Coffee looked up and saw an opportunity. He yelled out, "Art, this way. We can get in. Come this way!"

Coffee tugged Cormier as the two men pushed through the crowd and entered the stadium. Cormier lost a sandal. Both men were breathing hard.

Kicked and slammed in their faces, Bruce Seeber and Rob Doremus carried on through the gauntlet and slipped inside. But, Leonard Eastman and Paul Galanti, the next pair, were obstructed.

An old woman screamed, "Ganti, you die!"

Eastman and Galanti were surrounded. The two Americans, swinging their free arms and shoving people away, made one last lunge over the pile of human beings and bounced through the gate.

Paul Galanti, new to the prison scene and in severe pain, talked out loud as he gasped for air.

"I hope we don't do this every week."

A few guards formed a wedge that opened a path to the gate. Skip Brunhaver and Jerry Singleton and Ed Davis and Jim Hivner, in another surge, saw the gate open and shut, then open again only a few inches. Working together within the wedge, moving forward while fighting all the way, each pair managed to slide through the narrow opening into the stadium. Hivner noticed a big bump on Davis's head. He had sustained a blow from a large rock.

Vietnamese rabble-rousers sat in the lower bleachers and ran around the infield while excoriating the Americans. Pistol shots rang out inside the stadium. The North Vietnamese military were ridding the area of the riff-raff that found a way inside.

Ron Storz and Wes Schierman, side-by-side, fought their attackers off with punches and kicks as they moved forward. Near the end of the line and approaching the stadium, they too met the frenzied pack.

Pushing, punching and shoving, Storz and Schierman, climbing over fallen people, fought through the demon-possessed crowd and reached the gate. The two men pulled the people away from it with their free hands as the mob roared. The two Americans fought the last of their attackers and passed through the opening. Wes Schierman managed a big smile, even a laugh.

Alan Lurie and Darrel Pyle, at position number twenty-four, right behind Storz and Schierman, fought hard and passed through the opening.

Jim Bell and Ralph Gaither, the last pair in the parade, still outside the stadium, were alone and isolated, the exact concern Bell had at the beginning of the march.

The two men paused for a brief second and pondered their chances of survival. Jim Bell breathed in deeply as hands grabbed him and Gaither to rip them apart. Due to a shoulder injury that had not healed completely, Bell was in acute discomfort as he spoke to Gaither.

"Ralph, I don't know how, but we gotta get through this madness."

Ralph Gaither turned his head slightly to the left and spoke evenly and unequivocally.

"God be with us. Let's go."

The mob, knowing Bell and Gaither were the last two American prisoners and now alone, immediately struck with extreme viciousness.

Both men had earlier recited the *23rd Psalm*. They did so again for the last forty feet of the march.

Ralph Gaither, pressing forward, began. "*The Lord is my Shepherd; I shall not want.*"

Bell continued with him, "*Yea, though I walk through the valley of the shadow of death, I will fear no evil . . .*"

Bell and Gaither reached the gate but could not pass through. The gate was closed. Three young Vietnamese attacked Ralph Gaither whose right hand was free. He struck back with a straight punch connecting with a face. Another man, swinging, took his place. Jim Bell, remembering Nga Nam, stepped in front of Gaither and slugged the guy hard with his left hand, connecting with the assailant's jaw. The pain in Bell's shoulder was on fire. Bell was attacked from behind. He countered with his left elbow.

The gate remained closed for what seemed an hour. Whatever number of persons outside were pushing it shut, denying Bell and Gaither entrance, as many people from inside were pushing it open to let them in. For a long time, the angry masses surrounded them and, without respite, accosted them while shouting for their death.

The gate opened slightly. With his free left hand, Jim Bell grabbed the gate's edge and pulled himself over the human pile toward it. Then, he used his left hand again, like a hammer, to beat people off. It was his best weapon for self-defense.

Both men recited the *Psalm's* final verse as they fought with their attackers. *"Surely goodness and mercy shall follow me ... and I will dwell in the house of the Lord forever."*

Bell crammed through the narrow opening. Ralph Gaither was right behind. Others pulled Bell and Gaither inside the stadium. The last two Americans escaped the clutches of the mob.

Bleeding, but now inside, Jim Bell and Ralph Gaither, their arms and legs scraped, immediately collapsed in relief and exhaustion while the stadium gate slammed shut for the last time.

Neither of the two men anticipated the strength David's biblical psalm gave them.

Outside Hang Day Stadium, in the streets of Hanoi, now void of any foreign prisoners, the mad bedlam and churning turmoil of the shouting, frothing Vietnamese didn't stop, but there was nothing more to see. No longer were there any Americans to attack.

The Hanoi March had come to an inglorious, disgraceful end.

In this classic photo seen worldwide in many publications, the two POWs in the forefront are the fourth pair in the march behind Robbie Risner and Everett Alvarez. They and the pairs behind them are, *left to right*: Pop Keirn and Kile Berg; Bob Shumaker and Smitty Harris; Ron Byrne and Larry Guarino, Dick Ratzlaff and Bill Shankel. Because of this photo, Bill Shankel was identified by his relatives confirming his POW status, whereas before he had been listed as MIA. *AFP/AFP via Getty Images*

Hayden Lockhart (*left*) steadies Phil Butler (*right*) after Butler has been hit in the head with a bottle of beer. *AFP/AFP via Getty Images*

Jerry Driscoll (*left*) and Tom Barrett (*right*) during the march. *AFP/AFP via Getty Images*

Onlookers express their anger at the Americans during the march. Photo taken at the beginning of the march on Trang Tien Street. *AFP/AFP via Getty Images*

THE HANOI MARCH

PART FIVE

WITNESSES

THE HANOI MARCH

CHAPTER 24

ANH AND QUI, CUONG AND HIEP

Nguyen Phuoc Thanh Anh studied cinema in Paris where he came to enjoy the French language, culture and of course, the wine. Paris was by all measures exciting and enchanting, an experience he never thought possible for himself. So enthralled, Anh took to wearing a beret and scarf. After his training, Anh returned to Hanoi where for the next fifteen years, he pursued a career as a film director.

Just before noon, on Wednesday, 6 July 1966, Anh received a hand-delivered invitation to film an event that night involving captured American pilots. Aged thirty-nine, Anh was one of four official government photographers who would document the show, a once-in-a-lifetime opportunity.

Anh and Phan Chat Qui, a colleague, prepared their movie and light equipment and ensured they had plenty of reels of new film. At 5:00 p.m., Anh and Qui attended a briefing at what used to be called the Metropole Hotel on Ngo Quyen Street. The two photographers learned they would be witnessing a parade which would soon begin at the Hanoi Opera House and terminate at Hang Day Stadium.

In place by 7:00 p.m., Anh and Qui, their equipment connected to a power source, waited on the top step leading to the opera house, a perfect vantage point from where they could film the start of the event.

Anh had attended many performances at the opera house. His wife sang there for Ho Chi Minh when she was a teenager. The interior ornamentation and acoustics were equal to those of Le Palais Garnier in Paris.

After sunset, the procession began. With film rolling, Anh trained the movie camera and his lights on the lead pair of prisoners as they came into view.

With only a few outward shows of hostility toward the Americans, the surrounding crowd, although noisy, was orderly.

The line of Americans continued to pass Anh and his assistant. Soon, Anh was anxious to relocate along historic Trang Tien Street to film more of the drama. Anh wanted to move beyond where the other photographers were filming.

Elsewhere, Kien Cuong and Hu'u Hiep, two friends unrelated to Anh and Qui's assignment, had just arrived at the intersection of Trang Tien and Hang Bai Streets, not far from the opera house. The main boulevard was lined with a thick mass of people on both sides. The crowd and the noise were overwhelming. People chanted at the top of their voices.

"*Trung tri nhung ten toi pham chien tranh My!*" ("Punish the American war criminals!")

Cuong and Hiep, like so many onlookers, stepped off the curb onto the pavement. Not more than five feet separated them from the exhibited Americans. Cuong screamed loudly at the lineup, "You are pathetic people."

Then, gesturing crudely toward the prisoners, Cuong turned to Hiep. "And these are the big, invincible American pilots?"

Meanwhile, Anh and Qui, carrying their movie equipment, shifted from the opera house to the intersection of Hang Khay and Ba Trieu Streets.

The lead pairs of Americans eventually approached the movie

makers' position. Attacks on the prisoners increased. Anh, continued to acquire film footage of the scraggly men and the riotous crowd.

A young woman from the countryside, a rifle slung over her shoulder, was standing a few feet from the curb. Someone held her back with a warning she would not be safe. She pushed the person to one side as she adjusted her rifle's sling. "Don't interfere, I want to see the American enemy monsters."

She turned to a militiawoman standing behind her. "They're so arrogant and proud. But look, they're trembling all over."

Anh and Qui jostled for position to take movies with bulky hand-held cameras. A media truck carrying mostly East European photographers paralleled the prisoners on their left, but soon disappeared.

When the last of the captives reached the transition from Hang Khay Street to Trang Thi Street, a large crowd screamed at them while throwing objects. Several people leaped into the street, struck the prisoners and immediately jumped back. One woman pushed forward and yelled to the crowd in a cackling laugh, "These Americans are terrified of us!"

Not far away, Cuong and Hiep, ignoring a distant air raid siren while watching the parade, stood holding bottles of beer in their hands.

Having vacated their position at the intersection, Anh and Qui, out of breath from running and lugging film equipment, arrived at the gated entrance of the driveway to the national library as it intersected the march route near Quang Trung Street. To their consternation, they discovered the lead pairs were already well beyond the entrance to the library grounds. They decided to move on and proceeded to Hang Day Stadium.

Cuong and Hiep left the bar and stood on the sidewalk on Pho Trang Thi. As each pair of prisoners passed, the two young men threw bottles and other debris at the Americans. Stepping off the curb, they kicked at several of them. The two friends soon left for the stadium area so as not to miss their last chance to assault the Americans.

Anh and Qui, now at Hang Day Stadium, set up their movie and light equipment. They plugged a long electrical cord into a generator nearby.

The paired prisoners turned left off Pho Nguyen Thai Hoc and angled toward the stadium. The first few scruffy Americans were nearing the end of the route. Anh and his colleague began filming.

A man yelled, "*Quan va dan mien Bac doi giac My den toi!*" ("Northern soldiers and citizens demand the American pirates pay for their crimes!")

The area outside the stadium gate was awash in anarchy. A large, boisterous crowd congregated just in front of the gate. The pushing and shoving caused people to lose their balance. Many individuals, bruised and bleeding, fell. Shoes and other belongings, now lying on the street, created walking hazards.

Anh, handling his camera, saw the American prisoners struggling to make their way to safety inside the stadium. They leaped over a mound of writhing bodies. The bystanders, taking advantage of fewer guards, descended on the American pairs, kicking, hitting and beating them but the Americans passed through chaos into the stadium.

Cuong and Hiep, now on the other side, intoxicated by the beers they drank and emboldened by the excitement of the crowd, attacked the Americans. They punched the prisoners and kicked them in their shins. Then, they retreated to the curb where they continued with verbal abuse while shaking their fists.

Finally, the last pair of captured airmen, fighting their way through the wild melee, entered the stadium. The crowd did not immediately dissipate. Rioters stood outside calling for American blood. Those who had been knocked down, staggered to their feet and stumbled away in a stupor. Anh and Qui were surprised by the ferociousness that had engulfed the prisoners.

Not wanting to miss any after-events, Anh and Qui returned to the opera house. Perhaps a tribunal or a formal accusation would take place there, but nothing happened.

The raw film footage was shown the next evening.

CHAPTER 25

TRAN THI NGOC TRAC

A fifteen-year-old girl born in Nghe An Province, Tran Thi Ngoc Trac, now living with her mother and father in Dong Anh, across the Red River north of Hanoi, heard about a spectacle scheduled to take place in the city that evening, the sixth of July. Her parents and two uncles, who resisted the government's previous decree to evacuate, went into downtown Hanoi on the noon bus.

Trac was told to stay home. Under no circumstance was she to venture out of the house. There was no reason why she should be in harm's way. This was business meant for adults, not for a person as young as her.

Trac's burning curiosity, however, drove her to disobey her parents.

The teenager could not understand why she should be excluded. Afterall, her parents were there and if trouble broke out, even they may not come home. What's the difference?

Trac disguised herself with a hat and shirt borrowed from a friend. She put her long hair up inside the hat. Twenty minutes later, Trac, choosing a back road, caught a ride on a military truck from Dong Anh to Cau Long Bien (ex-Paul Doumer Bridge) at the edge of the Red River.

One week before, the Americans bombed a target just north of

Gia Lam Airport, south of where Trac lived. Black smoke rose into the sky for days. Surely, Cau Long Bien would be an eventual target for American aircraft.

Trac stepped onto the steel-truss bridge, the longest bridge in Vietnam, the pride of Hanoi, and began the perilous, two-kilometer journey across the wide river. She stopped for an instant at mid-section of one of the bridge's imposing spans to enjoy the stateliness of the structure. She looked down on Bai Giua, an island splitting the Red River into two short channels. She saw air defense soldiers milling around anti-aircraft gun emplacements.

Trac carried on across the bridge, arriving at the Hoan Kiem area at the north edge of the lake at five pm. She was hungry but food was scarce. A small street restaurant served her leftover pho in a porcelain bowl.

Beyond Hoan Kiem Lake, a huge, noisy crowd gathered. They were lining Pho Trang Tien from the opera house. Trac learned the street was crowded all the way to Nga Nam. She asked a shop keeper what the spectacle was all about and was told American air pirates were to be put on display for the public. Trac had never seen an American. She heard they were bigger than giants. Without question, she had to see for herself.

Trac rounded the lake and walked past the Bu'u Dien (Post Office) and turned left on Trang Tien Street to be at the front of the crowd.

Now, standing on some steps, she had a good view of what may transpire. Employees from the bakery opposite her on the other side of Trang Tien Street stood waving their arms and shouting. Their clothes and caps were dusted with flour.

The plaza in front of the opera house to her left was dimly lit. Commotion was constant. Trac heard loud voices coming from the far side of the opera house but she couldn't make out what was being said.

Soldiers created a gap in the crowd from which tall, haggard Americans, dressed in prisoner uniforms, standing side-by-side in pairs, came into view.

A motorcycle led the procession as the prisoners rounded a circle in front of the Hanoi Opera House in a counterclockwise manner. The lead pairs, having walked three-quarters around the plaza angled down Trang Tien Street, west toward her position.

A military officer holding a bullhorn while riding in a motorcycle car, spoke in Vietnamese and in English.

"You show respect. You creemeenal aggressor."

Photographers filmed and snapped pictures.

Chants began and a few items were thrown at the American prisoners, but the display, with armed guards present, was, for the most part, peaceful. Trac felt safe. She could not understand why her parents were so concerned.

The first several pairs of prisoners were now in front of Trac. The Americans were indeed large men. The guards kept their bayonets pointed in toward the prisoners. Other guards yelled at the prisoners and in a couple of cases, physically assaulted them.

A woman screamed as she gestured emphatically.

"Risna, you not good! We hate you!"

Another woman called out as she pointed an extended finger to the man's companion who she recognized from newspapers in 1964.

"Aser-ves, you blood pay. Must die!"

Someone else yelled, "Avrez, sonbitch!"

More prisoners approached Trac's position. She was astonished at the number of American prisoners. They were tethered at the wrists by manacles or rope. The prisoner uniforms appeared old and worn. They hung ghost-like on the scruffy prisoners who continued to trudge past her.

Trac found an opening and stepped to the curb. She turned her head to the right and saw one American protecting himself from a guard who hit him and climbed on his back.

The bullhorn continued loudly while behind her, agitators incited the crowd.

Screaming people hurled debris at the American pilots from

curbside. Trac saw what she soon realized were arcs of human spit. Trac thought for a moment, then acted. She walked just to the outside of the guards and made her way through the crowd to the intersection of Trang Tien and Hang Bai Streets where young people often gathered at night.

The loud crowd continued their unruliness. Shouting men threw objects while women, shaking their fists, chanted, "Americans are beasts!"

A woman rushed past the guards. She hit the prisoners with her pointed hat.

A bottle hit a prisoner while a rifle butt smashed into the back of his mate's head. Both men staggered on their feet. One fell to the ground only to be picked up by his companion.

A woman yelled, "Look, they're so weak!"

A man yelled as he pointed to a pair of Americans, "Sonna-bitch pigs!" He spit in the prisoners' faces. "You never see USA again!"

A military officer pushed the man back, but the man yelled again in spite. "We are the victors with our foot on your heads now!"

The onlookers far outnumbered the guards and, gaining courage by their strength, began to accost the procession at will. The guards were losing ground.

Trac felt she had to do more than watch. She yelled out while she shook her fist.

"Nguoi My xau xa. Chung toi khong can cac anh!" ("Americans no good. We don't want you!")

But compared to the woman next to her, her comments were benign.

"Bon My den day giet hai dan Viet Nam!" ("You Americans come here to destroy Vietnamese people!")

The noise increased as everyone screamed in unison at the prisoners: "American imperialists sonbitch! We don't want your bombs!"

An old man yelled as best he could in a sputtering voice, "Down with the American aggressors who have caused much sorrow and suffering in our country."

An unshaven man walking with crutches and wearing an old Viet Minh uniform yelled out.

"*Khach my khong moi! May sau hon bon Phap!*" ("Unwelcome American guests! You are worse than the French!")

Then he exclaimed his hatred in the simplest of terms. "*Bọn may chet!*" ("All you scum, die!")

Trac looked directly at an American and shook her fist.

"How many of our people have your bombs killed?"

With so much noise, Trac was sure her voice was not heard. Trac yelled louder at the prisoners. "You must pay blood!"

To her right, part of the parade, now past her on Pho Hang Khay, slipped into the dark void beneath the big trees next to the southern tip of Hoan Kiem Lake and disappeared from view. From her left, the line of American prisoners kept coming. The noise level rose.

The crowd intruded into the parade. Photographers were pushed aside. One man fell and dropped his camera. The assault of thrown debris and garbage increased. Trac hoped the air criminals would be hit. But, being so close, she feared she may be struck as well. She stepped back onto the sidewalk next to the lake.

"Where are they going?" she asked a man standing next to her.

"Stadium Hang Day," the man responded.

Trac questioned: *Should she go there?* Trac recalled the worry her parents expressed earlier in the day. But Trac had come this far. She was compelled to continue on. Now drawn into the spectacle, she had to see the conclusion.

Trac left her place next to the lake and, walking quickly with short runs, proceeded toward Hang Day Stadium. She fought through the crowd only to reach the impassable congestion of Nga Nam where she took an alternate route to her destination.

Trac arrived not more than twenty minutes later. All around her, frenzied people anticipated the end of the parade and the harm they hoped to inflict on the American airmen.

As the disoriented prisoners approached the stadium, a mass of humanity closed in and descended on them. The mob beat, kicked and hit the Americans with objects. The guards, what were left of them, protected themselves, not surprisingly, more than they did anyone else.

The gate to the stadium was barely open. It couldn't open any further since it swung out into the vengeful mob. Some people had fallen on top of one another causing the prisoners to leap over the bodies.

Trac yelled, "*Giac My!*" ("American pirates!")

Trac screamed again, "*Diet My!*" ("Americans die!")

As each pair of Americans approached the gate, sometimes several pairs in a surge, the same mayhem occurred. The crowd could not be controlled.

Trac could not bear to watch any more of the pandemonium. She shrank away from the crowd to a side street. The yells, taunts, noise and raucousness of the crowd continued. Trac left the area for fear of being hurt, but now afraid of encountering her parents, walked quickly toward Cau Long Bien. She made her way back across the Red River, then caught a ride to Dong Anh.

Now home, Trac went straight to her room. She lit a mosquito coil, drew the netting around her bed and curled up under a sheet. Her parents would return soon. Trac had to pretend to be asleep but disturbed by what she experienced, her body shaking, she didn't sleep.

Tran Thi Ngoc Trac would never forget this night.

PART SIX

ANTECEDENT AND FALLOUT

THE HANOI MARCH

CHAPTER 26

DAH, DAH-DAH-DAH . . .

Beginning in 1964, long before the Hanoi March, North Vietnamese officials, using strongarm measures, interrogated and tormented the captive American airmen continuously. They wanted information about their air operations. However, the technical data an aviator may provide as time passed, would lose value. Once an aircraft carrier left the Gulf of Tonkin and Air Force squadrons rotated home from Thailand, neither now a threat (although replaced with others), what could captive airmen originally assigned to those entities be forced to give their captors that would be of benefit? They were pilots who knew something about past missions but nothing now about new ones. They weren't strategists or policy decision makers.

Tied up immediately after capture, beaten black and blue, starved, dehydrated and eventually taken to Hanoi, each American was subjected to the same tirade. Who are you? From where did you come? How Many planes? What kind of planes? Who was your commanding officer?

The Americans divulged nothing. The American code of conduct for military personnel proscribed an American prisoner from divulging information beyond the big four (name, rank, birthdate and serial number). The North Vietnamese, however, gleaned information about each mission and captured pilot from international news reports, magazines and other sources.

The North Vietnamese knew much about each pilot: To whom he was married, number of children, his home town, even what his parents did for a living. The Vietnamese also might learn an individual flew from a certain aircraft carrier. Quick research through various sources revealed data about that carrier (length, speed, number and types of planes, its air wing, even when it left its home port). While such operational information was interesting, one underlying piece of intelligence was highly sought by the North Vietnamese: When will Hanoi be bombed?

Interrogators became equally desirous of propaganda material. Always wanting bio information and self-incriminating statements, often through the most injurious methods, the Americans were tightly controlled, interrogated and often beaten by men half their height, who relished dishing out pain to achieve their objectives. Restrained in leg irons while locked in steel and concrete cells barely as wide as a person was tall, the Americans would sit or lie for weeks in their own repugnant excrement. Some would be placed in solitary confinement without food or water for extended periods of time.

The fortunes of notoriety for a few of the American prisoners did not work in their favor. Their importance was not lost on the interrogators. The North Vietnamese did not fail to exploit the fame of some of the Americans now residing in Hanoi's prisons.

The antecedent of things to come began in September 1965, ten months before the Hanoi March.

The Americans at the Zoo saw an immediate change in atmosphere in the prison camp and demeanor in camp personnel. Security improvements were ramped up, rations cut. Guards became more mean-spirited, officials stiff and robotic. Routines and protocol tightened up.

Vietnamese guards discovered Robbie Risner, then at the Zoo and a senior ranking officer, had previously declared a nine-point directive to his fellow prisoners. Risner instructed the men to collect anything useful, follow the code of conduct, always communicate, learn names of other prisoners and their locations, maintain constant surveillance and attend church.

The Vietnamese, needing to squash incipient leadership among the Americans, condemned Risner's directives. They quickly published a camp regulation list in response. Do not communicate, show polite attitude, answer all questions, obey instructions, do not try to escape and, most notably, "All criminals must bow to officers and guards!"

Further, to disrupt the prisoners' organization, Fox, the Zoo camp commander, issued punitive orders to remove Risner. He was taken to Hoa Lo and placed in leg irons for forty-five days. He was often tied up, gagged with pieces of newspaper and beaten.

Another American, one of the first to undergo predetermined beatings as part of the interrogation, was the RIO of Ralph Gaither's Navy F-4. His name was Rodney Knutson. Along with Robbie Risner, Knutson would endure unbearable suffering near the end of October 1965.

During long periods in leg irons while blindfolded, Knutson was kept in seclusion at starvation levels for days. Knutson had the presence of mind to realize the North Vietnamese were intent, not so much to obtain information, but merely to break his will. A hard individual, Knutson resisted, which frustrated prison officials

The North Vietnamese, changing technique, increased their wicked efforts. Using Knutson, they refined their cruel, unique form of bondage.

Made to lie on his stomach, Knutson's buttocks were so beaten with a fan belt, his entire backside was a raw, bloody mess. He was made to sit on his bleeding wounds on his concrete bed with his legs placed again in leg irons at the foot of the slab. His arms were tied tightly behind his back. The pain was excruciating. But there was more.

A rope was tied to Knutson's arms and the other end looped over a hook above where he sat. Pulling on the end of the rope, his interrogators lifted Knutson's body up off the concrete slab.

The action rotated his arms up and forward and his head down toward his knees. He was suspended with his legs still in irons. His arms rotated out of their sockets. The whole weight of his body was now hanging from the tendons and muscles in his shoulders.

At intervals, the interrogators tightened the suspension rope. Knutson's arms swelled to twice their size, turned red then purple, then black. All feeling left. Knutson, valuing his life, knew he could not live much longer.

Release from the ropes should have brought relief but the immediate rush of blood back into the veins and arteries of Knutson's arms and legs produced a stinging, electrifying sensation so painful, he screamed out in debilitating agony. Nerve endings, painfully reawakened, would take weeks if not months to heal.

Surprisingly, all the Vietnamese seemed to care about was Knutson's background. He gave them a farcical account of his life back home. He was allowed to shower and was taken back to a cell where, completely exhausted, Knutson slept for the first time in days.

Rod Knutson, without realizing it, experienced the first evolution of what came to be referred to as the "rope trick." More than just tying one's hands up, the victim's arms were tied so tightly behind his back, his elbows and forearms touched. He was seated on the floor with his legs extended and locked in leg irons. His trussed-up arms were rotated forward over his shoulders while his head, forced forward and down, touched the floor between his knees. His teeth often scraped the concrete floor while his arms were pulled from their sockets.

Ron Byrne didn't escape the madness. Toward the end of 1965, Byrne was taken to some room in an undisclosed building where he faced three American activists. They grilled him aggressively, even obnoxiously, on a number of points. Byrne didn't respond to their inquiries and resisted their putting words in his mouth. He didn't give them anything. Byrne soon experienced the evolving rope trick.

Evidence of American prisoners being subjected to ruthless

beatings in Hanoi was first revealed to the international community by Jeremiah Denton in late spring of 1966.

Denton, an accomplished aviator and thoroughly trained in military sciences, was expert with airborne electronics and aviation technology. He piloted the A-6 Intruder.

Since the A-6 was an advanced aircraft. Jerry Denton and Bill Tschudy, the first A-6 crew to be captured, proved a fortuitous shootdown for the North Vietnamese who wanted to know all about the aircraft.

Denton encountered the Rabbit with whom he had many arguments, jousts and unpleasant harassing verbal exchanges. He also experienced encounters with Dog, Cat and Mickey Mouse.

In April 1966, Denton, hounded around the clock for three straight days, refused to write a letter of confession. The Rabbit told him if he did not cooperate, he, like Robbie Risner, would be taken to Hoa Lo. He would meet a new person, a professional in coercive techniques. The Americans soon called that person Pigeye.

Through continued interrogation involving the rope trick, Denton almost died. He was forced to write a statement but found he could not hold a pen. His hands didn't respond. He made spiraling motions on the paper.

Later, Cat told Denton he would be meeting with the press. He must be polite and do as he was told.

Within a few days, Denton, escorted by the Rabbit, Cat and Mickey Mouse, was led to a room in an unknown building and seated in front of a Japanese film crew. The interview began first with accusations levied against the Americans about the immorality of their military interventions, which Denton dodged. Eventually, the film session turned to innocuous topics such as whether he was given cigarettes and allowed to wash.

Bright camera lights shining directly into Denton's face made him squint and blink. Denton, thinking quickly, realized the glare may work to his advantage. He could send a message out to the world.

Denton, looking straight into the camera, blinked in a sporadic, but systematic, determined cadence.

American intelligence analysts would try to make sense of what they were seeing during a showing of the film in the USA later in June. Such strange eye movement—maybe his eyes hurt—but in an epiphanal moment they understood. Denton, using Morse Code with his eyelids, signaled *dah, dah-dah-dah, dit-dah-dit, dah, dit-dit-dah, dit-dah-dit, dit.*

Jeremiah Denton, the A-6 pilot from Alabama, had spelled out a seven-letter word: T O R T U R E.

Later, after the Hanoi March, Vietnamese lust for the airmen's statements of regret or contrition rose to a crescendo. The interrogators were obsessed with persuading the Americans to admit their war crimes. They tried to force each prisoner to sign his name at the bottom of pre-written statements renouncing the United States and to compose letters to congressmen and senators denouncing the war. Better yet, each American must express his sorrow and, in a letter to Ho Chi Minh, ask for forgiveness. The North Vietnamese, however, weren't having much luck.

Drawing on perfected techniques, the North Vietnamese revised their interrogation procedures. No longer were the Americans roughed up, made to stand for hours and days, slapped and cuffed about the ears and denied food or water while placed in leg irons. Other heinous measures, beginning with the rope trick, were in the offing. Unlike the march, nothing would be revealed to the public.

The American prisoners, isolated and totally on their own, soon endured, to the full extent and on a continual basis, what Rod Knutson initially experienced and what Jeremiah Denton blinked out two months before.

During the late evening of 6 July 1966, after the Hanoi March, the North Vietnamese at the Zoo contented themselves with spontaneous, alcohol-induced fun at the expense of the hapless Americans.

Bob Purcell gave the event an ironic name. He called it the "garden party."

CHAPTER 27

GARDEN PARTY AT THE ZOO

The horror visited on fifty Americans, starting at the Hanoi Opera House at the head of Pho Trang Tien, Hanoi's famous main street on 6 July 1966, ending two hours later in mob mentality and unmitigated violence at Hang Day Stadium, was inconceivable. It represented a continuation of wanton abuse that resulted in even more hideous maltreatment.

The American prisoners, breathing hard, covered in sweat and sickening saliva from the two-hour ordeal, were seated in a line on the cinder running track inside the stadium.

Each person, having come through hell, sustained cuts and bruises on his arms and legs. Many had cuts on their faces. Blood ran from noses and mouths and coagulated on skin and clothes. Racing blood pressures and heart rates in each man slowly normalized. Adrenaline continued to flow through the men's bodies, causing some to shake.

The Americans felt their wounds and rubbed their eyes and sore muscles. Stunned, thirsty and in slight shock, they had one other thing in common: they survived the march.

Those American prisoners who participated in the Hanoi March and others who didn't were not out of danger. As a result of the march, the North Vietnamese, assured by their presumed success, became exceedingly aggressive toward the Americans. To some, this was nothing new. It had been going on for some time. The fallout would be worse.

Rabbit, the orchestrator of the Hanoi March, walked among the seated prisoners inside the stadium. His dialect still betraying him, Rabbit raised his bullhorn.

"You sheen anger Vietnam people. Want you die."

Disregarding the Rabbit, Everett Alvarez, breathing hard, asked Robbie Risner whether he was all right.

"Yeah, doing OK," Risner responded with his usual calm. "And you?"

"I'm good, Robbie. Bruised but OK."

Risner smiled.

"We gotta recover."

Rabbit continued with his exhortations as he walked among the seated Americans.

"You cause crimes against Vietnam people. You creemeenal pirates. You now know."

Larry Guarino, his insolent voice dropping as he spoke, couldn't help but react.

"Crap. Know what?"

Alan Brunstrom, never at a loss for humor, smiled as he wiped the sweat from his face.

"Whadaya know? We're not going home after all," he said. "Imagine that."

Trucks, their engines running, were lined up inside the stadium to return the Americans to their respective prisons. While the truck rides to Hoa Lo and the Zoo were easy, the ride to Briar Patch, thirty-three miles northwest of Hanoi, over bomb-damaged roads, was arduous. Interestingly, on the way there, Jim Bell, peering from beneath his blindfold, was shocked. There were no guards in the back of the truck!

The Americans exchanged stories of the ordeal and questioned what was next as they headed to Briar Patch in the dark without benefit of headlights. The conversation turned to escape; the code of conduct urged them to make such an effort. It was their duty.

The men decided any attempt to jump from the unguarded truck bed would be suicidal. They were, after all, handcuffed. If not killed in the fall, they would be easily captured before sunrise and probably shot. Retribution on others would be harsh.

But retribution was exactly what the North Vietnamese had in mind in the first place.

Upon their return to Briar Patch after midnight, Skip Brunhaver and Jerry Singleton, one by one, were taken to interrogation. The guards had free reign to do whatever they wanted. Both men sustained multiple hits, lots of body bashing and face slapping. They were put in the ropes until forced to write something. Neither man offered an apology, but rather, each contrived disjointed incongruities. Suffering from the effects of the ropes, they were returned to their cells.

Bill Tschudy was told that because of his bad attitude during the march, he would suffer the consequences. Tschudy didn't understand. How can this be? All he did was march with the others. Nevertheless, he was taken to Hoa Lo the next day for "attitude improvement." Tschudy didn't return to Briar Patch for several days. During his short time at Hoa Lo, the North Vietnamese roughed him up badly.

The trucks to the Zoo, immediately after the march, arrived much sooner than the trucks to Briar Patch. The worn-out occupants regained their composure during the trip by making light of what they experienced. The guards, also fatigued, were not so strict. A strange humor erupted among the returning Zoo prisoners.

"Do we get a reward? Ice cream?"

"Hey, Coffee, don't you wear shoes?"

Someone told Art Cormier he looked better now than before the march.

Dick Ratzlaff spoke up.

"See that guard stick his bayonet in Groucho's butt?"

"Yeah, near Guarino and Byrne," Duffy Hutton said.

Laughing, Ratzlaff continued, "Ole Groucho . . . he bled pretty good."

The march through Hanoi did not satiate Fox, the Zoo camp commander, or interrogators. If anything, the march signaled a greater hell for the prisoners. Officials and interrogators were going to make a point if for no other reason than intimidation, torment and entertainment. They already had plenty of practice beginning with Robbie Risner, Rod Knutson, Ron Byrne and Jerry Denton months before.

The prison authorities instructed the guards to beat the shit out of the American criminals. The guards, enjoying bottles of *Bia Hoi*, happily obliged.

A filthy swimming pool filled with old film cans, garbage, debris of all sorts and stinking green slime was the centerpiece of the Zoo's courtyard and also served as a toilet. The American captives referred to it as Lake Fester. After the march, Americans were tied to trees near the foul-smelling pool, then mercilessly beaten until the next morning.

Bob Purcell became sick to his stomach when he heard screams of sheer terror from the pool area as a result of the new horror being imposed on his countrymen. He knew he would soon be in the same predicament.

The Vietnamese were determined to make the American prison leadership cave in.

Still feeling stiff from the numerous assaults he sustained during the march, Alan Brunstrom slipped under his mosquito net. The cell door opened and Brunstrom was taken from his cell by three guards.

Dragged outside, Brunstrom was forced to join the party. His arms were wrapped backward around a tree trunk and tied securely. He was gagged. Guards came around all night and kicked Brunstrom hard and punched his face and tormented his legs. They pushed a gag into his throat. Not enough, they opened Brunstrom's mouth wider, stretching his face muscles. They jammed the gag farther down his throat with a stick, breaking his upper denture. Brunstrom, barely able to breathe, heard his teeth crack-

ing. Beaten beyond sense until the next morning, the torturers removed the gag from his throat. Brunstrom, coughing as he gasped
for air, was untied from the tree. His body, the consistency of jelly,
collapsed. Brunstrom was dragged back to his cell.

Howie Dunn and his marching partner Ray Merritt were made
to sit blindfolded with their backs against a tree on opposite sides.
Their arms were wrapped backward around the tree. Dunn's hands
were tied to Merritt's hands. Rags were crammed into their
mouths. Each man almost choked to death as they were beaten.
After several hours of being slugged in the face and kicked, Dunn
and Merritt, at the end of their endurance, were released from the
tree and taken back to their cell blocks.

Pop Keirn, tied around another tree, gagged and beaten, was in
serious pain from the severe kicks to his groin. Keirn was left tied
to the tree for two days. He almost died.

Bob Shumaker was also tightly blindfolded but his arms were
not secured around a tree trunk. Instead, the guards tied his arms
behind his back and made him walk at a pace faster than normal.
BAM! Shumaker, blind, walked into a tree. Stunned by the impact,
he fell backwards to the ground. The guards, laughing boister-
ously, picked Shumaker up and made him walk again, this time,
straight toward a block wall. The impact knocked him out cold. He
woke up later in his cell.

The guards, amused with their treatment of Bob Shumaker, focused on Robbie Risner. Blindfolded with his hands tied behind
him, Risner was aimed at a parked truck. Risner reeled from the
collision and hit the ground. The guards stood him up and pointed
him at a set of steps. Naturally, Risner tripped and immediately
fell forward, slamming his face flat on the concrete.

Arthur Cormier had been tied around a tree and slapped, hit and
kicked. He passed out but was revived only to be beaten again until
the get-out-of-bed-gong sounded throughout the camp later that
morning. Untied from the tree after sunrise, Cormier went to interrogation, what the Americans referred to as "quiz," two times that day.

At the noon session, Cormier told Fox and Dum Dum if they had another crazy parade or outdoor torture session, someone would probably be killed. Cormier was beaten senseless.

That night at 9:00 p.m., Cormier endured his second quiz. Dum Dum insisted Cormier confess his war crimes. The Vietnamese beat him when he refused. Cormier maintained his innocence.

"I didn't do anything. I was a medic in a rescue helicopter."

The North Vietnamese put Cormier in the ropes that were ratcheted up so much, all blood flow was cut off. The pain was piercing. He had to try something else, invent another scheme. He devised an internally-conflicting statement.

"I was a passenger in a slow-moving, completely unarmed helicopter with no ordnance when it bombed all of North Vietnam."

Dum Dum, living up to his nickname, looked dumbfoundedly at Fox, then, without expression, back at Cormier. Fox lit a cigarette. He thought for a moment as the smoke swirled around his head, then motioned for Cormier to be removed. Cormier, off the hook, was returned to his cell.

Cormier smiled about a side incident where Dum Dum uttered what sounded like nonsense: "Cheek-uh-goo."

Cormier, caught off guard, looked up inquisitively. "What?"

Dum Dum asked Cormier whether he was pronouncing it correctly. Cormier, suddenly realizing what Dum Dum was trying to say, laughed in agreement.

"Go ahead," Cormier said. "Pronounce Chicago any way you want. I don't care." Dum Dum, pleased with himself, smiled.

Jerry Denton's arms had been wrapped around a tree. His hands were tied to another American prisoner. A dirty rag, some of it still protruding from his mouth, was stuffed deep into his throat. Denton fought for air, but realized his time on earth may be up. Using residual air in his lungs, Denton coughed out his initials: "JD." A surprising response came back from the other side of the tree: "JC."

Denton wondered, *"What the...?"*

Had Denton's prayers been answered? Confused for a second, Denton realized it was Jerry Coffee who was also gagged. Both men survived the ordeal.

Neither Larry Guarino's ego nor his feisty Italian-American pride were eroded during the garden party. Guarino, untied from Ron Byrne before sunrise, was free of the tree. He was led to an interrogation room.

Once in the room, the Vietnamese took advantage of Guarino's weakened condition. Three interrogators faced Guarino.

"We show last night America can be defeated by Vietnam. American people will rise up against your war."

Then, they wanted to know what Guarino thought of the march. Guarino responded.

"What you've done will be condemned by the United States. American people will never tolerate such conduct against its airmen. My country will demand retaliation."

The interrogators persisted.

"Greeno, you must help us. We encourage you to cooperate."

Indignant, Larry Guarino, a longtime officer in the United States Air Force who had proudly fought in Italy and Korea, wasn't having any of this business. He retorted derisively.

"Cooperate with what?"

Guarino, the oldest American prisoner who participated in the Hanoi March, nonplussed, sat back in the chair. "Naw, shit. I ain't gonna help ya."

Guarino was beaten to within an inch of his life. Barely able to stand and bleeding from his injuries, he was thrown back into his cell hours later.

Like Guarino, at first light on the morning of 7 July, Bob Purcell was taken to quiz. Percy always stayed one step ahead of the Vietnamese. Weeks before, Percy, risking his life, had climbed across roof rafters to drop food to a prison mate who, immobilized by leg irons, was starving.

Now, the prison officials wanted confirmation from Purcell: Did he see the determination on the faces of the Vietnamese people during the public exhibition?

"Yeah, I suppose . . . kinda dark . . . I guess," Percy said.

After a short session of physical abuse, Purcell, to his utter amazement, was thrown back in his cell.

Later, Percy, pre-empting Spot, who stood in front of him in Percy's cell, asked what caused all the fire and black smoke on the horizon on the twenty-ninth of June. Spot explained it was the result of American air pirates bombing churches and schools. Purcell, knowing these were never targeted, but playing along with the ploy, looked at Spot incredulously.

"You know," he said, "it'd be a good idea if you stopped storing fuel and oil in churches and schools."

Spot, wide-eyed at such cheekiness, blurted out.

"How you know about oil?"

Purcell, now knowing he had the upper hand, if only for a moment, shrugged his shoulders.

"Criminy," Percy said with obvious sarcasm. "You think I don't know what an oil fire looks like? I've bombed petroleum facilities and know an oil fire when I see one."

Spot stormed out of the cell, slammed the heavy door and locked it.

In an incident separate from Purcell's, on the morning after the march, Wendy Rivers, who underwent severe punishment during the garden party while tied to a tree and still suffering from those injuries, was awakened early by loud tapping sounds on the wall.

Rivers had his own insouciance

The North Vietnamese sometimes gave each prisoner a ration of cigarettes. One day a couple of months before the march, Rivers consumed his allotment. He whispered to Ron Byrne, in the next cell, through a tiny hole that Robbie Risner had previously managed to poke in the wall. Byrne slipped Wendy three cigarettes through the hole. Byrne didn't hear anything afterwards, but soon, he saw cigarette smoke being blown through the hole into his cell. Rivers, displaying his humor, was thanking him.

The urgent tapping sounds that Rivers heard continued louder. Bob Shumaker, recovering from his collision with a tree and a solid wall, and Smitty Harris, who also endured the garden party, were calling him.

Wendy Rivers had smiled fearlessly while dodging bottles, rocks, rotten fruit and fists in the middle of the Hanoi March. Now, he smiled again at the friendly sarcasm of Shumaker and Harris who, using the tap code on the wall, sent their message.

They demanded Rivers not invite them to anymore of his birthday parties.

Born on 6 July 1928 in Seward, Nebraska, Wendell Rivers turned thirty-eight the day of the evening he, Shumaker, Harris and forty-seven other Americans strolled through the streets of Hanoi and later, attended a garden party.

THE HANOI MARCH

CHAPTER 28

BEER, COURTESY THREE ENEMY MIG PILOTS

Before the return of the prisoners to their camps and the resulting garden party at the Zoo, Cole Black, nursing his wounds at the stadium, was quick to question whether arrival at the gate at the end of the march was preplanned or if it was an emergency because the crowds could not be controlled.

Chuck Boyd, sitting on the stadium infield next to Black, intruded on his mate's thought. He figured it was a good opportunity to teach Black the tap code. Black was a new shootdown and he would need it.

"Cole," Boyd whispered. "The tap code's easy. Eliminate K and arrange the remaining twenty-five letters in five rows . . . A, B, C, D, E . . . first row. Fifth row is V, W, X, Y, Z. The letter B is signified by one tap, first row, two taps, second letter. Tap . . . Tap, Tap; letter B, got it? It's simple. That's how we communicate. You'll have to learn the acronyms. GM is good morning. V means Vietnamese and . . ."

Chuck Boyd was abruptly interrupted.

Guards untied and separated Cole Black from Boyd. Vietnamese medics, only a few of which were on hand, treated Black's wounds with mercurochrome that stained his face and clothes. Later, while the Vietnamese were consumed with fun at the garden party, Cole Black experienced something else.

Black should have been returned to the Zoo with Chuck Boyd. Instead, he was driven by jeep to Hoa Lo. He was led through the tunnel just beyond the main entrance, then left into a plaza and shoved through a door. His arms now free, Black found himself in the knobby room, so-called because of hundreds of plaster nodules protruding from the scarred and stained green walls, ostensibly to absorb sound.

Black was told he would meet high-ranking officials. The next day, the door opened. Three men with no discernable military rank entered and were immediately shocked by what they saw seated before them.

Cole Black was nothing short of a wretched mess. Blood, still dripping from his chin and lesions on his face, soiled his prison garb. The stain from the medicine administered at the stadium made him look even more despicable. His lacerated lips were swollen. Cut so wide open during the march, Black could stick his tongue deep into his lips' wounds.

The visitors were disgusted by Black's filthy appearance and repulsed by the oozing blood caking on his skin and drying on his clothes . . . as if he were to blame.

One man brought in a tray carrying three bottles of beer and a pack of *Truong Son* cigarettes. He placed the beers, obviously refreshment for the Vietnamese visitors, on the table. He asked the guard to leave, turned and addressed the ruffled, bloodied American. "You must show good attitude," he said. "Unnerstan?"

The three men, each one having lit a cigarette, began to question Black.

"You see MiGs?"

"A few."

"Where?"

"Here and there."

"How fast you fly?"

"Dunno. Not that fast."

"How you carry missiles?"

"Shit if I know, I don't load 'em."

The men wanted to know if he had ever been involved in low altitude aerial combat.

"Maybe. Not sure."

Black concluded by the questioning and rhetoric consistent with aviation lingo that the three men were fighter pilots. Black recalled the day he was shot down. A MiG split-S-ed away from him at low altitude and smashed into the ground. Black thought North Vietnamese pilots had not been trained for low-level dogfights and did not care to engage in ground-hugging aerial combat. Now, they sat in front of him trying to pick his brain.

Cole Black didn't give them any information.

After thirty minutes, the three men, frustrated by Black's reticence, stood up and began to leave the room. In a last-minute gesture, one man slid the pack of cigarettes and unopened beers across the wood table to Black and motioned for him to drink up.

Cole Black, like any red-blooded American fighter pilot, quickly opened the bottles and gulped the beer before they were confiscated. Although the bottles were not exactly cold, the beer never tasted better. Black spent two more days in the knobby room.

On the fourth night, Black was taken back to the Zoo in a jeep and told to go to his room. Black found it odd that he was happy to be back in familiar surroundings of the Zoo, regardless of how dismal his so-called "room" was.

Rat, an interrogator, entered his cell and, in a friendly tone, asked Black if there was anything he wanted. Surprised by the conciliatory gesture, Black said he wanted to wash the blood off. Rat allowed him to wash up and clean his clothes.

During his first "liberty," two weeks after his shootdown, Cole Black, often blindfolded, wearing soiled pajamas, met angry Vietnamese people, took a truck ride, saw Hanoi while participating in a ridiculous spectacle called a parade, dodged airborne debris and a few rifle butts, got the hell beat out of him, lost a lot of blood, learned Smitty Harris's tap code from Chuck Boyd, then drank beer in the knobby room at Hoa Lo courtesy of three enemy MiG pilots.

Totally bizarre!

CHAPTER 29

MINISTRY OF JUSTICE

Two days after the Hanoi March and the garden party, Ray Merritt was taken from the Zoo to Hoa Lo where he was put into a small cell. A day later, Merritt was escorted out the main prison doors above which were the words Maison Centrale. He was taken across Hoa Lo Street to the Ministry of Justice building, the old French courthouse, and ushered into a large room. Vietnamese officials sat on the opposite side of a long table.

The Rabbit spoke to Merritt.

"Do you know why you are here?"

"No."

Merritt was told he must sign a confession and write a statement declaring America's illegal involvement in North Vietnam.

Merritt shook his head. "Not gonna happen."

An air raid siren sounded. The officials left the room for shelters while guards remained. The guards forced Merritt to the floor and placed him in the ropes in the usual position. When distant bombs exploded, the guards kicked Merritt in the ribs repeatedly.

The interrogators eventually returned to the room to find Merritt gagged and in the ropes on the floor. The guards continued to kick him which caused his throat to choke when he reacted. His face was pressed to the floor with his arms rotated over his shoulders. Merritt, passing in and out of consciousness for over a day, could not tolerate the pain any longer. As the Vietnamese began to untie him, Merritt, about to pass out again, knew he would be forced to make some sort of statement.

Once out of the ropes, Merritt shook severely from his bondage release. His arms spasmed as blood flowed back into the veins and arteries. Merritt was given a pen and some paper. His limbs, painfully re-awakening from the effects of the restraints, were un-usable. Merritt could barely hold the pen. The quality of his pen-manship was less than a child's.

What Merritt eventually wrote was arcane and simple-minded, but it worked. Cleverly worded, the almost indecipherable scribble, rambling and nonsensical, was hardly a conciliatory statement; and it was certainly no confession.

CHAPTER 30

MAKE DECISION WRONG, BAD HAPPEN YOU

Participating unwillingly in the Zoo garden party, Duffy Hutton was tied to a tree with occasional bouts of being clobbered, slapped and kicked. But, for a surprising unknown reason, the North Vietnamese didn't beat Hutton to the extent they did others.

Hutton was taken to Hoa Lo with Ray Merritt. Two days after Ray Merritt's torture, Hutton was escorted across Hoa Lo Street to the Ministry of Justice where he met the Rabbit. Hutton was told he had to compose letters condemning America. He must publicly apologize for his crimes.

Hutton, staring at his nemesis, uttered two words: "No way."

Several guards were called in. Hutton was tightly tied up and beaten. Restrained on the floor, trying to hide his pain, Hutton didn't scream, which angered his guards. His situation became worse.

Vietnamese interrogators procured a rope and ladder. They made a noose, placed it around Hutton's neck and secured it tightly. Then, climbing up the ladder, they slipped the other end through a steel hook protruding from the ceiling from which an electric fan normally hung. They took the rope's free end and ran to a corner which tightened the noose even more around Hutton's neck. The North Vietnamese yanked the rope, snapping Hutton off the floor until his body was almost dangling free. His captors were hanging him!

Hutton, still hopelessly tied up in the ropes, his vision blurring, felt the strain on his neck and jaw. The mounting pressure on his brain, the sensation of restricting claustrophobia and the lethal effects of suffocation overwhelmed him. With his eyes rolling to the back of his head, his vision going blank, Hutton quickly passed out. The Vietnamese slackened the rope just in time. Hutton hit the concrete floor hard. Regaining consciousness, Hutton's eyes opened slightly.

The guards removed the gag. Rabbit asked Hutton if he was prepared to cooperate. Hutton, now fearing for his life, looked at his torturers and nodded his head.

Rabbit probed him quizzically.

"You refuse before and now you agree. I not unnershtan. Why you ready to write now, but not before?"

Hutton looked at the Rabbit.

"Are you insane? I can't tolerate any more of your shit torture."

It was a situation in which any response was incorrect.

The Rabbit, a cynical smirk crossing his face, was not satisfied with Hutton's "absurd assumption."

"If you think you were being tortured, you are clearly wrong."

The Rabbit, taciturn, sat back in his chair while staring at Hutton. "We will have to continue with questions until you show good attitude."

"You're damn crazy," Hutton said. "I almost died." Hutton caught his breath. "Your people tried to kill me!"

"But you not be kill, you not die," Rabbit said with a smile.

Hutton responded along the lines that what must have occurred then was a case of friendly persuasion.

Again, the wrong response.

Hutton made up his mind to relieve his suffering by killing himself. He wanted to crawl to a stone protrusion at the bottom of the wall to bang his head against it, but found he could not crawl at all.

Hours later, Hutton was freed from the ropes. His arms were on fire. The pain was too much. He was surprised at all the blood on him and more surprised to see the blood he left behind on the wet floor.

As a result of the march, the garden party and the current abuse at Hoa Lo, Hutton's blood-covered face looked as if a butcher had worked on it. His vision was impaired and his right eye, swollen shut, sagged. His facial muscles failed to respond. The right side of his face was paralyzed. His neck, rubbed raw, was burning from the tightness of the noose.

The Rabbit pointed to a sheet of paper on the table in front of Hutton, now seated in a chair. He withdrew a pen from the pocket of his uniform and tossed it on the table.

"Now, air creemeenal you."

The Rabbit continued pointing. "Must write letter apology. Unnershtand? You write!"

Duffy Hutton didn't compose an apology letter or any letter intimating he was a war criminal, nor did he sign anything.

Returned to the Zoo and now back in their cell, Ray Merritt and Duffy Hutton along with Cole Black, communicated with other American airmen about their ordeals at Hoa Lo.

A tapped message came back to Merritt, Hutton and Black.

H-I-T, followed by *G-B-U*. Hang in there. God bless you.

To date, North Vietnamese weren't netting much.

Physically forced to beg for mercy, or to request leniency, each American prisoner faced egregious, prolonged torture. The horrifying program continued for years. The new torture program just about killed each man. In fact, many met such a dire fate.

The Rabbit, unfazed by those consequences, reminded the Americans on several occasions: "Do thing right and treatment good happen. Make decision wrong, bad happen you."

THE HANOI MARCH

PART SEVEN

RETROSPECT

THE HANOI MARCH

CHAPTER 31

CONUNDRUMS

The Hanoi March, the control of which the Vietnamese failed to maintain, and the residual excitement cruelly manifested in the garden party and at Hoa Lo, were gratuitous acts of extreme brutality carried out by a mobster gang.

But why the march in the first place? What was the reason?

To Rob Doremus, the march was something that happened out of the blue. The men were taken from their prison cells, paraded through Hanoi and returned to their cells a few hours later—just another day.

Years later, Larry Guarino, echoing his thoughts on 6 July 1966, commented openly. "The Hanoi March was strictly a propaganda piece for the media and in fact it was no big deal . . . a non-event, pure bullshit."

Paul Galanti's impression was similar to Guarino's. The march was a spontaneous, meaningless demonstration on the part of the North Vietnamese.

Oddly, the North Vietnamese, convinced of their cleverness, yet desirous of confirmation, were eager to learn of the American prisoners' impressions of the march.

After the garden party, Jerry Denton was taken to quiz where Fox questioned him, but not before he was told to wipe the blood from his face. Fox wanted to know what Denton thought of the march.

"You're a bunch of fools," Denton responded. "You'll never get away with this."

Fox was taken aback by Denton's candidness. He fell quiet. Then, Fox smiled coyly.

"Let me tell you something, Denton, that you should never forget."

Fox, explained to Jerry Denton the march was not the idea of the Quan Doi (Army), but rather the idea of the citizens.

"It was a stupid idea," Denton said. "No one will be impressed."

"The people wanted it," Fox said.

"So what?"

Fox stared at Denton, then replied, "You don't understand what I am trying to tell you."

Denton responded without hesitation.

"You've made a big mistake."

Fox continued his explanation, but with a slight twist.

"People throughout Vietnam want more. They are demanding criminal Americans be returned to the province in which they were captured to face trial and execution."

Denton knew such a move on the part of the North Vietnamese would dilute Hanoi's control. He thought he may be witnessing a rift between the Communist party and the army of North Vietnam. To Denton, the march was an appeasement in response to local demand.

"You're completely nuts," Denton retorted.

Fox lit a cigarette. He was not amused.

Robbie Risner recalled later that the Vietnamese provided not so much an outright reason, but rather a hint of their justification for the march through loud speakers, each referred to as a liar's box, part of the scratchy prison intercom system. He and others were reminded that the march revealed the hatred of the Vietnamese people. The people demanded their blood as retribution.

But of course, the liar's box lecture didn't stop there. It assumed a different slant. The prisoners were warned to confess their crimes and cooperate. Otherwise, they would die. As the Rabbit continued to emphasize, choose good or wrong path, Ho Chi Minh or President Johnson, leniency or death.

On 7 July 1966, the day after the march, Hanoi Hannah took to the airwaves with her ludicrous propaganda contrivances.

"A strange thing happened yesterday. The Americans were being taken to interrogation and bystanders saw a parade."

For Hannah, at that moment completely off the mark, the parade must have been just a conveyance.

On the same day, an article in *Quan Doi Nhan Dan* (Army People's Daily) read:

> *"Hanoi burst with victorious pride for the destruction of seven aircraft and the capture of American aggressor pilots during the past week."*

Events of the past week were not without their own history.

Months before, on 24 December 1965, President Johnson ordered his second bombing halt. The North Vietnamese took advantage of the standdown and sent more troops and equipment south. At the conclusion of the ineffective halt on 30 January 1966, American air forces were back in strength.

In April 1966, the joint chiefs submitted a plan to the U.S. secretary of defense for a strong air campaign against North Vietnam. Execution of the plan, principal of which was the destruction of fuel storage, would cause the North Vietnamese to reconsider their militancy.

The secretary sent the report and his recommendations to the president. The entire scheme was scrapped.

As fate would have it, on 23 June 1966, the Air Force and Navy received approval to attack the petroleum, oil and lubricant (POL) storage sites at Hanoi and Haiphong.

The plan was cancelled two days later.

On 28 June, to the amazement of military officials, approval was given again for the strike to proceed. The mission was to take place the following day.

Major James Kasler of the 388th Tactical Fighter Squadron based in Takhli, developed operational plans for the U.S. Air Force to attack the POL facilities in Hanoi. On the Navy side, Lieutenant Mike McGrath of Airwing 14 on the USS *Ranger* (CV-61), prepared plans for the Haiphong attack.

On the morning of 29 June 1966, commanders of the Navy strike force were surprised to learn news of the impending attack had been made public. The enemy's air defenses were undoubtedly ready.

Still, the U.S. strikes were executed as planned.

During the raids, the President of the United States, sitting on the edge of the bed in his upstairs White House bedroom, waited anxiously late at night for news.

The news came. Contrary to Hanoi's later claims, the daring raids were a complete success.

Black, oily smoke, the same smoke about which Bob Purcell asked Spot, rose in dense columns from each storage site to twenty thousand feet or more leaving a telltale sign of the strikes.

The Air Force and Navy lost only one plane, an F-105 Thunderchief. Murphy Neal Jones, a twenty-eight-year-old Air Force captain from Baton Rouge, Louisiana, was the pilot.

Severely injured, Jones parachuted to earth and was immediately captured in Gia Lam.

That same evening, the Vietnamese drove Jones, his left arm in a sling, through Hanoi. Hysterical crowds surrounded the truck in the back of which he was forced to stand.

In April, one year earlier, Smitty Harris, shot down while bombing the infamous Ham Rong Bridge, was paraded on foot amidst angry crowds through the streets of Thanh Hoa while tied to a slow-moving motorcycle.

Word of the exhibition of Harris undoubtedly reached Hanoi and, coupled with Jones's truck ride, must have added support for a grander display to show North Vietnam's outrage to the world.

Like the Soviets parading German prisoners through the streets of Moscow in 1944, the North Vietnamese presumed a spectacle, a follow-on to the exhibits of Harris and Jones, would be a perfect propaganda tool.

The headlines of *Nhan Dan (People's Daily)*, the Vietnamese labor party newspaper, another periodical, also on the seventh of July, stated:

> *"Victorious Hanoi clearly sees firsthand the enormous defeat of the American Air Forces. Punish the American war criminals."*

The lengthy article continued with an interesting comment.

> *"It could be said that every American aircraft carrier and every base in the South and in Thailand . . . has representatives in Socialist Republic of Vietnam prisons."*

Quan Doi Nhan Dan was less cryptic in its prescient assertion:

> *"Tomorrow the Americans will continue to come here. We will clip their criminal wings."*

Over the next six years, many more American "representatives," including the planners of the 29 June POL raids, would have their wings clipped and end up in Hanoi's prisons. Indeed, on the day of the Hanoi March, Major James Young in an RF-101 was shot down and captured.

Ironically, the same 7 July *Nhan Dan* article revealed the direct link between the raid on North Vietnam's major POL facilities and the march.

> *"Yesterday, 6 July, exactly one week after our resounding victory, the people of Hanoi witnessed a special spectacle related to the devastating defeat of the American air forces."*

As a result of the surprise POL raid, planning for the march, to take place one week later, was urgent, amateurish and ad hoc.

Jeremiah Denton, widely read, a graduate of Annapolis and later George Washington University from where he received a master's degree in international affairs, drew a correlation between the physical surroundings and the crowd's demeanor during the march.

Denton was not the first observer of the phenomenon associated with crowds. In 1895, Gustave le Bon published his seminal work on crowd behavior. He advanced his contagion theory whereby an individual in a crowd who acts in accordance with the crowd is not the same person when alone. The influence of the crowd is so great as to alter a person's reasoning, behavior and demeanor.

Denton specifically observed that at the very beginning of the march, the architecture appeared erudite and upscale. The citizens, reflecting the sophistication of the immediate area, were well-dressed, their demeanor composed and respectful. The ambiance of the neighborhoods deteriorated along the way. At the end, the environs were far cruder and the demeanor of the people, peasant-like and shabby, nastier. In Denton's mind, the relationship between sophistication and demeanor was directly proportional.

Evidence confirms the number of marchers was originally intended to be fifty-two. Rodney Knutson and Harlan Chapman were slated to participate in the march. On the morning of 6 July 1966, sandals and prisoner uniforms with a number on each shirt were issued to the two men. They were told "put on and wait." However, they were caught communicating with another American during the day. As punishment, Knutson and Chapman were "denied the pleasure" of marching with the others.

The start of the march, the route and its terminal point were selected due to the history of Trang Tien Street and ease of access by the local people

The criteria used to select the American prisoners for the Hanoi March seemed to revolve around mobility and outward health, but a mystery remains in another regard.

Forty-nine of the marchers were officers. Why not all fifty? Art

Cormier was the only enlisted man on the march while other officers were available.

None of the Americans showed any contrition during the march, nor did they make any display of acquiescence. They remained bold. This exacerbated the anger of the Vietnamese who, mistakenly, were satisfied they had broken the will of the American airmen and hopefully the United States. Surely, America's leaders would cease their aggression toward the Hanoi government. Ill-conceived, the whole plan failed.

The European press received special access to film the march. The international exposure would make the American prisoners demand an immediate end to the war, a complete slip-up on the part of the North Vietnamese. Their strategy didn't work.

The march would highlight just how humanely the Americans were being treated. This part didn't work out very well either.

The Hanoi regime clearly regarded the Americans as essential to their bargaining position. More valuable alive than dead, the North Vietnamese, too casual, even careless with their march preparations, miscalculated and stupidly placed their most treasured asset in mortal jeopardy at the hands of the citizens.

Washington interpreted the public display of the herded Americans as a disturbing indication that Hanoi would stage a show trial.

The United States contended that American aviators must be protected by the 1949 Geneva Agreements.

Hanoi argued that since there was no declared war, the agreement did not apply to the American prisoners. The North Vietnamese relegated them to common criminals.

President Johnson stressed to Hanoi that its actions were contrary to international law. Plus, the Americans held in North Vietnam were military men who followed orders. They were not criminals.

Two months after the Hanoi March, a guard told JB McKamey to "make ready." McKamey and others were going on another march. Four hours later, the guard came back laughing explaining to McKamey that he was making a joke.

THE HANOI MARCH

CHAPTER 32

AFTERWORD

Almost seven years after the Hanoi March, the men who participated in the event were paired up in Hanoi again, but not for a parade through its hostile streets. They were going home.

Overall, during the course of the war, North Vietnam captured and incarcerated four hundred ninety-five American servicemen in its prisons. Twenty-eight of these men died in captivity due to brutal treatment. Four hundred sixty-seven airmen were released in small batches over several years, but the vast majority during the first quarter of 1973.

Midmorning on 12 February 1973, one hundred sixteen prisoners including forty-nine out of the original fifty Hanoi marchers were driven in buses from Hoa Lo to Hanoi's Gia Lam airport. The Americans were shuttled out of North Vietnam to Clark Air Force Base, Philippines, on C-141 cargo planes, the first of three leaving at 12:30 p.m. Subsequent flights followed till the last American left Hanoi at the end of March.

Sadly, Ron Storz, the fiftieth marcher, died in captivity of mysterious causes. His remains were returned to the USA in 1974.

Darrel Pyle died in a plane crash in Alaska also in 1974.

Murphy Neal Jones, driven through Hanoi in the back of a truck on 29 June 1966, was released with the others on the third flight on the twelfth of February.

The men wore new but ill-fitting clothes, shoes and jackets. Each man carried a tote bag the North Vietnamese provided. Some brought out prisoner uniforms and a few mementos. The tin drinking cup was the most prized souvenir.

Duffy Hutton celebrated his forty-first birthday in Hanoi the day before his release in 1973. His mates made him a crude cake from cocoa mix found in the contents of relief packages. They decorated it with M&Ms.

Jim Hivner, Bob Purcell, Skip Brunhaver and Jerry Driscoll celebrated birthdays within days of their release. Weeks later, Kile Berg, Ralph Gaither, Jerry Singleton, David Hatcher and Alan Lurie would also celebrate birthdays in freedom.

Being the first returning prisoner to be reunited with his family, Alan Brunstrom fondly recalls hearing for the first time in years on 25 March 1973 his teenage daughter say to him, "Happy Birthday, Dad."

Brunstrom has always thought that had the march proceeded another block, some Americans would have been killed.

Smitty Harris was surprised when, just before his release, the North Vietnamese presented him with his wedding ring taken from him in Thanh Hoa eight years before. He had to sign a receipt.

Harris retired with his wife Louise to Tupelo, Mississippi. In 2021, he was honored with the official renaming of the Tupelo Post Office. It is now called the "Colonel Carlyle Smitty Harris Post Office".

Four men—Jon Reynolds, Robbie Risner, Alan Lurie and Chuck Boyd—rose to the rank of brigadier general in the U.S. Air Force with Boyd later becoming a four-star general. Chuck Boyd recently sold his T-34 aircraft that he flew in Virginia. The U.S. Air Force honored Robbie Risner with a statue of him on the grounds of the Air Force Academy in Colorado Springs.

On the Navy side, Bob Shumaker and Jeremiah Denton retired as rear admirals. Like Boyd, Shumaker often flies his private plane.

Denton won his seat in the U.S. Senate in 1981 representing the state of Alabama.

Bill Shankel was the first returning prisoner to marry after his return to the USA. Shankel had been identified in a photo as a result of the Hanoi March which transformed his status from MIA to POW. Eventually, Shankel became a medical doctor. Due to his attraction to the Southwest, he worked with the Navajo Indians in New Mexico.

Wes Schierman returned to the Seattle area and flew for Northwest Airlines until he retired. He and his wife had a third child, another daughter.

After retirement from the Navy in 1980, Everett Alvarez served as Deputy Director of the Peace Corps and later as Deputy Administrator of the Veterans Administration. He then started a federal contracting management consulting company.

Ron Byrne, long retired from the Air Force as a colonel, resides in Prescott, Arizona, where he keeps his mind active with on-line education.

Jim Bell's shoulder was reconstructed at Bethesda Naval Hospital after which he regained much of its use.

Immediately after his release, Paul Galanti made a second appearance on the cover of a national magazine—*Newsweek*—this time with his wife. He received rehabilitation treatment at Portsmouth Naval Hospital. He held senior administrative positions at the Naval Academy. After retiring from the Navy, Galanti served in the senior staff office of three professional associations for many years. In 2010 he was named Commissioner of the Virginia Department of Veterans Services by Governor Bob McDonnell.

Jim Hivner recounted one of his dearest memories of Ed Davis.

Hivner and Davis lived in the same cell at Briar Patch. Each learned the other was from Pennsylvania. They grew up not more than one hundred miles apart. They never stopped talking about their childhood experiences. Hivner would later write: "Hanoi March, bad, really bad. Roommate, good, really good!"

Ed Davis smuggled a puppy he named "Ma Co" out of Vietnam in his carry-on and brought it home.

Sadly, Al Brudno passed away of unfortunate circumstances a few months after his repatriation. Bob Brudno, his brother, succeeded years later in having Al's name engraved on the wall of the Vietnam Veterans Memorial in Washington, D.C. (Panel 05E, Line 02).

Tom Barrett remembers when the Briar Patch camp commander allowed Al Brudno to sing a Christmas carol on the camp radio just before Christmas 1966, months after the Hanoi March. Brudno sang "Puff the Magic Dragon." So moved, Barrett memorized the song's lyrics and to this day sings it during his morning walks as a tribute to Brudno and others.

Art Cormier completed his college education and became an officer in the U.S. Air Force, then retired to Maine. Rob Doremus was assigned to a Navy recruiting station in Ohio where he retired. Porter Halyburton retraced the route of the Hanoi March in November 2008 and is currently busy in North Carolina writing his memoirs. Dick Ratzlaff also retired to North Carolina. Jerry Coffee retired to Hawaii; Bob Peel, Art Burer and Wendy Rivers to Texas; Bruce Seeber to Louisiana; Ray Merritt, Cole Black, Bill Tschudy, who appeared on the cover of *Time* magazine in December 1970, and Phil Butler retired to California, Larry Spencer to Iowa, Len Eastman to Maryland and Render Crayton to Arizona. Howie Dunn retired to Colorado. Larry Guarino, Pop Keirn, JB McKamey and Hayden Lockhart retired to Florida, Paul Kari to Ohio; and Murphy Neal Jones to Delaware.

As of this writing, twenty-five Americans who participated in the Hanoi March still survive.

* * * *

In Vietnam today, the Hanoi March is all but forgotten.

Hanoi has undergone major transformations including high rise office buildings, a new international airport and an expressway into town across the Red River on an imposing cable-stayed bridge, the new pride of Hanoi.

The old Long Bien Bridge, what the American airmen knew as the Doumer Bridge was attacked in April and December 1967 and destroyed. Repaired, but in poor maintenance, it still functions today, carrying only light traffic.

More than half of Hoa Lo prison, the Hanoi Hilton, was razed after the war to make space for tall apartment buildings. Coincidentally, Cole Black and his wife Karen visited Hoa Lo in 1994, the day demolition began.

The remainder of the prison is now a museum. The knobby room still exists and now contains part of the American prisoner display. Few visitors know the room's sordid history.

All that remains of the Zoo is the main gate. Much of Briar Patch has been dismantled.

The Hanoi Opera House was restored in the late 1990s as part of a deal with Hilton Hotels and Resorts to build a *real* Hilton in an adjacent property in Hanoi. The location where the marchers assembled, next to the new hotel, became a crude car wash. The area is now a public park. The roundabout in front of the opera house is still there.

The Metropole Hotel has been expanded and modernized, but it retains its early elegance and charm.

Trang Tien Street or Pho Trang Tien (ex-Rue Paul Bert) remains much as it was. Congested with shops and overrun with pedestrians, cars and motorcycles, Pho Trang Tien is still revered as Hanoi's main avenue.

Nga Nam is even more congested. Trains, as they cut across Pho Nguyen Thai Hoc, continue to barrel through town rattling the homes to either side. Hang Day Stadium was demolished and a new one built in its place. The layout of the surrounding neighborhood has changed.

The little sidewalk breakfast restaurants where Pho is served, the loudspeakers from which music and exercise instructions blare, Hoan Kiem Lake and its turtles, and the giant trees that deeply shade Pho Hang Khay still exist. Teenage boys still gather at the intersection of Trang Tien Street with Hang Bai Street on Friday nights.

Vietnamese prison officials such as Dum Dum, Owl, Groucho,

Dog, Mickey Mouse, Cat, Pigeye, Fox, Frenchy and Spot slid into obscurity. Nguyen Minh Y, notoriously known by the Americans as the Rabbit, continued his military career until the late 1980s. After that, he led a spurious, controversial international life until he died in the 1990s. In 1976, Trinh Thi Ngo, the infamous Hanoi Hannah, moved to Ho Chi Minh City (Saigon). She passed away in 2016.

The first C-141 to arrive in Hanoi on 12 February 1973, dubbed the "Hanoi Taxi," is on permanent display at Wright-Patterson Air Force Base in Ohio.

Soon, fifty years will have passed since the Americans returned from Vietnam. Penned by Wes Schierman in 1972, the last stanza of his six-hundred-word poem, "The Hanoi March: A Night to Forget," written in simple meter, is a poignant closing to the saga of 6 July 1966, if not the entire prisoner of war experience.

Behind windows barred
I hope it's worthwhile
The cost has been great
I'll try to forget
I'll try not to hate.

The individual and collective legacies of the Americans incarcerated in North Vietnam will remain forever. The tenacity, perseverance and the faith of each man that he would survive and come home is a testament to his determination and personal desire to succeed in life and be a positive force for family, faith, service and country.

The unity, valor and heroism of the Americans who participated in the Hanoi March are exemplified to this day by their personal dedication and professional accomplishments, their courage, and through an organization born in Hanoi proudly known as the Fourth Allied P.O.W. Wing.

They returned with honor.

Welcome Home.

Porter Halyburton stands at the intersection of the march route (Nguyen Thai Hoc Street) and the north-south railway which demarked the separation of Route Package 6A and 6B. Photo taken November 2008. *Author's collection*

Art Cormier in California in 2022. *Photo courtesy Art Cormier*

Paul Galanti, currently living in Richmond, Virginia, at the POW mini-reunion at Nam Viet Restaurant in Arlington, 2009. *Author's collection*

Ron Byrne, now living in Prescott, Arizona.
Author's collection

Smitty Harris at his grandson's wedding in
Alabama in December 2021. *Photo courtesy
Robin Harris Waldrip*

Jeremiah Denton in his Virginia home in 2009. *Author's collection*

Cole Black visited Hoa Lo in 1994 while on a trip to Vietnam with his wife Karen. Cole met a tragic fate in 2007 when the private aircraft in which he was a passenger crashed in southern California. *Photo courtesy Karen Black*

Rob Doremus in his recruiting office in Ohio in 1978. *Photo courtesy Rob Doremus*

Tom Barrett hiking with his wife Susanne in Pennsylvania in 2017. *Photo courtesy Charles Barrett*

Jim Bell (*right*) is seen here pinning Navy wings on his son Matt in Corpus Christi, Texas in 1989. Jim's grandson Hunter has also been awarded his Navy wings. *Photo courtesy Dora Bell*

Wes Schierman after his first solo flight in eight years in 1973, only months after being released from Hoa Lo prison. *Photo courtesy Faye Schierman*

Chuck Boyd in his T-34 aircraft in
Virginia in 2016. *Photo courtesy
Chuck Boyd*

Three POWs who participated in the march and who attended
the POW reunion in Colorado Springs in June 2021. *Left to
right*: Bill Shankel, Alan Brunstrom and Everett Alvarez. *Photo
courtesy Tom and Kathy Freeberg*

Bob Shumaker (*left*) with Everett Alvarez. Shumaker was the second US airman to be captured in North Vietnam. Alvarez was the first. Photo taken at a POW mini-reunion at the Nam Viet Restaurant in Arlington, Virginia in 2009. *Author's collection*

Larry Guarino in his home in Florida in 2011. *Author's collection*

Skip Brunhaver in 2019 at a gala honoring American POWs held at the Museum of Flight in Seattle, Washington. *Photo courtesy Skip Brunhaver*

Bob "Percy" Purcell in 1974 when he received his promotion to Air Force Colonel. *Photo courtesy Suzanne Purcell*

THE HANOI MARCH

ACKNOWLEDGMENTS

Great reliance for this comprehensive telling of the Hanoi March was placed on research conducted in the USA and Vietnam and on multiple, lengthy individual telephone and in-person interviews with each participant. Each man took the time to graciously share his experiences and guide me through the intricate details of the march.

In addition to the participants of the Hanoi March, I want to recognize other individuals who also assisted me with background, technical details, translations and graphics:

Bob Brudno
Bob Destatte
Hoang Tran Dung
Paul Mather
Mike McGrath
Agnes Raffier
Lori Schoening
Ray Stubbe

Recognition must be given to Suzanne Purcell who patiently and painstakingly transcribed Robert "Percy" Purcell's thoughts, narrations and answers to my questions; to Kathy Freeberg who helped her father Alan Brunstrom recount his memories; to Mary Berg for her assistance with her husband Kile Berg; to Susan Page Coffee who tirelessly assisted her husband Jerry Coffee with his recollections; to Emilee Reynolds who helped with Jon Reynolds's responses; and to Karen Davis, the wife of Ed Davis who provided valuable insight.

Special thanks to Dora Bell and Karen Black, wives of Jim Bell and Cole Black, respectively; and to Faye and Stacy Schierman, wife and daughter of Wes Schierman, who reviewed a draft manuscript and also offered their own input.

Also, I want to thank those who provided photographs for this book.

My gratitude to other individuals who provided independent critique of chapters and portions of early manuscripts.

Carol Jean Bolton
Betty Jo and Gary DeBusschere
Rodney Knutson
Harley Patrick
Gilbert, Mija, and Mido Raffier
Raymonde Rossi

Finally, I must thank Mike Archer, Larry Caster, Lee Humiston, Dan Jenkins, Wayne Johnson and Shirley Iwane, Barrett Tillman, Clark and Ruth Hawksworth and Natalie Cohen for their interest and encouragement, and *The Henry* for its warm, early-morning hospitality while working on various drafts of this book.

SOURCE MATERIAL

I am grateful for the personal accounts of the march found in the following books:

A P.O.W.'s Story: 2801 Days in Hanoi, by Larry Guarino
Beyond Survival, by Gerald Coffee
Chained Eagle, by Everett Alvarez
Code of Conduct, by Karen Black
Old Glory is the Most Beautiful of All, by Richard and Hazel Keirn
Passing of the Night, by Robinson Risner
Reflections on Captivity: A Tapestry of Stories of a Vietnam War POW, by Porter Halyburton
Tap Code, by Carlyle "Smitty" Harris
The Heroes' Wife, by Dora G. Bell
The Strength to Endure: A Memoir, by Paul Kari
Three Lives of a Warrior, by Phillip Butler
Two Souls Indivisible, by Fred Cherry and Porter Halyburton
When Hell Was in Session, by Jeremiah A. Denton, Jr.
With God in a P.O.W. Camp, by Ralph Gaither

Unpublished written accounts of the Hanoi March from the collections of Ray Merritt, Wes Schierman, Alan Brunstrom, Duffy Hutton and Tom Barrett were particularly informative, absorbing and captivating.

Five books proved invaluable to my understanding of the POW experience:

Honor Bound: American Prisoners of War in Southeast Asia 1961-1973, by Stuart I. Rochester and Frederick Kiley

In Love and War, by James B. Stockdale

POW: A Definitive History of the American Prisoner-of-War Experience in Vietnam, 1964-1973, by John G. Hubbell

Prisoner of War: Six Years in Hanoi, by John M. McGrath

Vietnam Air Losses, by Chris Hobson

The following books provided rich background information:

Bean Camp to Briar Patch, by John N. Powers

Dien Bien Phu, by General Vo Nguyen Giap

Dragon's Jaw, by Barrett Tillman and Stephen Coonts

Hanoi's War, by Lien-Hang T. Nguyen

Hell in a Very Small Place, by Bernard B. Fall

Leading with Honor: Leadership Lessons from the Hanoi Hilton, by Lee Ellis

Mad About the Mekong, by John Keay

North Vietnam's Strategy for Survival, by Jon M. Van Dyke

Strategy for Defeat, by U.S. Grant Sharp

To Hanoi and Back, by Wayne Thompson

Viet Nam: A Long History, by Nguyen Khac Vien

Equally important, specific information about the history of Hanoi and Trang Tien Street (Rue Paul Bert) was gleaned from excellent accounts by the authors of the following books:

Hanoi: Biography of a City, by William S. Logan

Hanoi: City of the Rising Dragon, by Georges Boudarel and Nguyen Van Ky

Histoire de Hanoi, by Philippe Papin

Old Hanoi, by Mark Sidel

The Transformation of Hanoi, 1873-1888, by Andre Masson (translated by Jack A. Yaeger)

Other valuable reference documents include:

A Mission of Vengeance: Vichy France in Indochina in World War II, by Martin L. Mickelsen

Mac's Facts (containing statistics about the POW experience) by John (Mike) McGrath

North Vietnamese Personnel Associated with US Prisoners of War (Declassified 1992), by the U.S. Defense Intelligence Agency

The Armed Forces Code of Conduct: An Examination of its suitability and application in the Vietnam War and in Future Armed Conflicts, by Ray Merritt, James Lamar and Robert Sawhill

The Tale of Two Bridges, by Glenn Griffith, James Jones, Keith Krause, Ronald Lord, Robert Martin, Malcom Winter and David Young

The Association for Diplomatic Studies and Training, Foreign Affairs Oral History Project: Interview of General Charles Graham Boyd, by Charles S. Kennedy,

United States Air Force Oral History Program: Interview of Col. Carlyle S. Harris, by Mark C. Cleary

Veterantributes.org website by Eric Anderson

I made use of the following sources as well:

> *Time* Magazine
> *Newsweek* Magazine
> *Life* Magazine

And from the Vietnam National Library, Hanoi:

> *L'Avenir du Tonkin*, monthly magazine published in Vietnam
> *Ngan Dan* (People's Daily)
> *Quan Doi Ngan Dan* (Army People's Daily)
> *Thu Do Hanoi* (Hanoi Capital)

ABOUT THE AUTHOR

G ary Wayne Foster has lived in and traveled to Vietnam a number of times, visiting such places as Hanoi, Da Nang, Khe
Sanh, Dong Ha, Thanh Hoa, Vinh, Hue, Dien Bien Phu and Ho Chi
Minh City. He took an interest in the Hanoi March and began writing about it in 2003. He has a BS degree from the University of California, Davis, and an MBA from George Washington University.
Mr. Foster lives in Phoenix, Arizona.

THE HANOI MARCH

OTHER BOOKS BY GARY WAYNE FOSTER

Phantom in the River: The Flight of Linfield Two Zero One – An account of a mission flown by a Navy F-4 Phantom II shot down over Thanh Hoa in 1967.

The President's Sandbox: A novel swirling around the Khe Sanh Terrain Model, based on real events in Washington, D.C., Hanoi and at Khe Sanh during the siege in 1968.

Launching Motor: A humorous account of an adventurous, ironic childhood experience.

Mr. Foster is currently writing about his six years living in Zaire (Congo) while working on the Inga-Shaba project in the late 1970s.

www.hellgatepress.com

Made in the USA
Columbia, SC
27 May 2022

61013750R00135